MW01195585

Reflections of Gratitude

David M. Seymon

WestBow
PRESS
A DIVISION OF THOMAS NELSON

WestBow Press books may be ordered through booksellers or by contacting:

WestBow Press
A Division of Thomas Nelson
1663 Liberty Drive
Bloomington, IN 47403
www.westbowpress.com
1-(866) 928-1240

Because of the dynamic nature of the Internet, any web addresses or links contained in this book may have changed since publication and may no longer be valid. The views expressed in this work are solely those of the author and do not necessarily reflect the views of the publisher, and the publisher hereby disclaims any responsibility for them.

Any people depicted in stock imagery provided by Thinkstock are models, and such images are being used for illustrative purposes only.

Certain stock imagery © Thinkstock.

ISBN: 978-1-4497-0625-8 (sc)
ISBN: 978-1-4497-0839-9 (e)

Library of Congress Control Number: 2011925888

Printed in the United States of America

WestBow Press rev. date: 05/10/2011

Dedication

This book is dedicated to my mom, Doris Selby; without her, I could not have been the man I have become. She has been with me from my beginning and saw me through all my travels in this wonderful, yet unique life I have led. She has been my source of strength in my quest for growth. My gratefulness is only exceeded by my love for her.

Acknowledgements

My ultimate thanks go to my creator, Jesus Christ, in allowing me to survive my ordeal and guide my hand in writing this book of inspiration and love. My gratefulness goes to my neurosurgeon, John R. Clark M.D., who, using his expertise, helped to make me the man I am today.

My family, friends, and acquaintances, all in their own way, assisted in many of my endeavors throughout my rehabilitative years.

A special thank you to our dear friend, Becky Shenton, for her valuable editing skills.

Lastly, to my loving 'newly wedded' wife, who, without her, this creation would never have been started, finished or even encouraged, go my love, respect and admiration for always being by my side.

David M. Seymon

Contents

I wrote a poem four months before my accident that seemed to foretell the whole incident. It is called

Premonition

As I look across a field,
    I see childhood memories
        Visions of harsh and pleasant experiences
            Run through the grass.
                I see life.
                    It is sitting in the unblemished corpse of a tree.
                        A bird?
                            A robin?
                                A gift?
                                    From God?
                                        From Him to me?
                                            Four faces appear,
                                                Four different roads,
                                                    Coming up the same trail,
                                                        I see a muddy path….
                                                            …It's the one I must follow.

Reflections Of Gratitude

by David M. Seymon

My first memory was when I was lying in what seemed to be a fortified bed with three heavy silver railings on each side. I was looking down with one eye at a near-skeletal body that was supposed to have been mine. It looked like a 'live' framework of bones, with those bones protruding out at every joint. A thin layer of skin covered them. I did not recognize this body, nor did I realize that I had four brain surgeries and been comatose over four months. The nutrients and medications given to me by the many nurses, 'angels of mercy', at the four hospitals I was in, helped to keep me alive. I also used this unconscious body as a vehicle for my survival.

The Growth Period

I grew up in a typical California middle class family with my mom, Doris, step-dad, Pete, two sisters, Leni and Gail, an Airedale terrier, Kelly, and plenty of energy. I played sports and received good grades in school.

My dad worked with his dad who owned a store, Fabric Lane, in San Leandro, California. When I turned thirteen, I worked there on Saturdays, from 8 a.m. to 12 p.m. As a stock clerk/custodian, I learned that when you work, good things come while earning the 'almighty dollar'. I saved enough for a car. It was our family's 1963 baby blue, Pontiac Tempest Le mans convertible. I paid $500.00 for it when I turned sixteen and old enough to drive.

My mom was always there for me. She was my consultant when I had problems as well as sharing my pleasures, my support in everything I did.

My two sisters were two and four years younger than myself. I seemed to favor the youngest more for an unknown reason. I just did. I am sorry now I did not treat them as equals. It could have been a hidden jealousy, but why? I thought I was number one. Now I realize that number one only meant being first born.

When I was in grammar school, I was a good student, played in all sports and games; football, basketball, baseball, even table tennis.

I wore braces on my teeth from the time I was seven until I was seventeen and a half. My goal, after I began wearing these lip hurting, cheek torturing, contraptions, with a headband, I had an overbite comparable to a mule's, was to become an orthodontist. My orthodontists, Doctors Thurston and Cheney, had the best cars, wore the fanciest, neatest clothes, and were the finest people you would ever want to meet on this planet. I liked them and I appreciated their way of being with youths; it seemed to keep them young and that is what I wanted!

I played catch with my dad, Pete, almost every night except Mondays, when he worked at his store, Fabric Lane, after dinner. When it was baseball season, we tossed the baseball; in football season, the football. We always threw more than only the ball: we tossed a lot of good talk between the two of us—what happened at school, any new kids there, and what I learned that day. I, in return, asked him about his work, his co-workers, and Opa, his father and the head of their fabric business. We also shared jokes we heard during the day. My dad loved to hear a good joke and he was a great joke teller. He had an excellent memory for those kinds of things. I could never keep up with him on that note. I tried, but, we all have our strong points! He never wrote many poems either.

At twelve, I went through a hunter's training course at Sears Department store and got my hunting license. My granddad, Eirwin F. Selby, mom's dad, took me duck hunting with my aunt's 20-gauge shotgun. I knocked down two, right out of the sky. We also brought home a dozen mud hens. Granddad had my first duck mounted. Boy, was I proud of my accomplishment.

Granddad taught me how to fish. We caught trout, bass, bluegill, and catfish. I went out on the San Francisco bay and caught a sand shark when I was 5 years old. Again, was I pleased! I even got my picture taken holding it. It was almost as big as me!

My friends and I played football up on the level portion of the street above our Hayward hills home. It was touch football where the eight- to twelve-year olds played. Without the pressures of today, back then, it was called 'fun'.

Puppy Love

I always liked girls even though my Granddad continually said, they were going to get me. I didn't understand what he meant. Every school year I would fall head over heels for one, usually making a fool of myself until I got their

3

attention. When I had them in my face, my mouth shut, I got frustrated and wanted to die but I got out of it, usually with a big silvery smile.

As a young teen, I never tried to kiss a girl 'romantically' until I was thirteen. My first 'real date' was with a thirteen-year-old young lady named Heidi. We went to a Job's Daughters installation where she was to become the Guide, first one on the 'totem pole' and she would progress up to the highest position, Queen. I had to wear a suit, tie and even polish my shoes for the occasion. That was a big deal for a tennis-shoe-clad kid. Her parents came and picked me up, took me to her installation in their 1963 brown Pontiac Bonneville. We sat in the audience and watched this ceremony take place. After it finished, we shared cake, ice cream and punch. Then, the music started.

I thank my dear mother, Doris, for 'trying' to teach me how to dance. I found out in a hurry I was no Fred Astaire, but learned enough to do okay. During the night, I even danced with her lovely mother, Betty. At the end of the evening, we came back to her folks' place, about half a mile up the hill from my house. Heidi's mom and dad got out of the car first and went inside while Heidi and I walked slowly up to the front door. I was NERVOUS; my dad had told me about his 'first kiss'. Well, I was all ready for the big event. I licked my lips, told her what a great time I had, put my arm around her waist, puckered up, and moved my head towards hers. She looked up into my eyes and then she softly screamed, "No!" and broke away and ran into her house. I stood there scratching my head, put my hand over my mouth, smelled my breath (it was fine), turned around, and walked home, dejected and puzzled. I said to myself, I should stick with sports, I will have better luck. I never told anyone about this incident until I grew up; how embarrassing!

The Bombshell

My dad informed the family we were going to move to San Leandro so he could be closer to his fabric store. My friends from Bret Harte Junior High threw a good-bye party for me at the Hill and Dale clubhouse up the hill from my home. We danced, said our farewells, and kissed. One girl kissed me sort of strange. she had her mouth open. It felt a little funny kissing and breathing at the same time, but it felt like I wanted more, open mouth smooching, what a novel idea. The weird thing about this evening was, I kissed all the girls and was not even a little bit embarrassed, but I *still* wanted to kiss Heidi, someday, maybe!

Finding Security

I lived in Hayward for seven years. We then moved to San Leandro, leaving all my old friends so I had to make new ones and dad could be closer to his business, Fabric Lane, a smart move for him but a 'serious' life change for me!

We moved on July 4th, 1965, into a five-level house a little over a mile from dad's store. It was an old English style home, but it had lots of stairs. I never had that many stairs in our home in Hayward except those coming up to the front, back and garage doors.

Marilyn

What a stroke of luck! It so happened, that one of the cutest girls in all of San Leandro lived right next door. Marilyn was a year older than me, which, at that time, meant there would never be a 'loving' relationship. We had a wonderful friendship and we talked for hours on end. She is one the finest people I could have ever wanted to meet. I love her dearly, still. Marilyn, Pam, Lou, Chuck and I used to go out and drink English 800 beer after some of our school basketball games, Chuck looked old enough to buy, a heavy beard helped. On the following Mondays, the girls started to call us names, all in fun. Marilyn called me 'Fish' and I called her 'Fish' in return. When one person saw the other in the school hallway and said 'Fish' first, they won the silly contest.

After my car accident, on one of my first visits from the hospital, I came home in my wheelchair; she visited me for the first time. She saw me and I started to say, f..f..f..f.. she had heard that people in comas, after coming out of that state, swear and curse so she thought I was going to say the big 'no-no'. I kept saying f..f..f..f,, then I blurted out in my 'Baby Hughy style' … 'Fish'.. After four months in a coma, I remembered to say, 'Fish'. Why would I have a memory of that when I couldn't even tell you what I had for lunch the hour before? That has to be one for the medical books.

When we moved to San Leandro in the summer, I signed up for a recreation league baseball. I rode my three-speed Schwinn bicycle up to San Leandro High School every game day to play ball with my new friends. I was a pitcher in little league when I lived in Hayward, and I continued pitching in this league throughout the summer. I made a friend, Louie, who eventually became as close to me any brother could be without being related. At the end of the summer, we entered eighth grade at Bancroft Junior High.

Coming to a new school, especially in eighth grade, is hard for a young teen. You have to make new friends all over again. Why is life so difficult at times? Lucky for me, I happened to have known the principal for about eight years prior to my moving. Mr. Larson was the father of one of my Hayward grammar schoolmates, Eric. They lived up the block from my family. He would have told my folks if I had done anything wrong at my new school, they had to be 'in cahoots' and I knew it.

Early Teenhood

Junior high was fun, but the junior highs in San Leandro and Hayward were different. In Hayward, the schools went from K-6, grammar school, junior high from 7-8, and high school from 9-12. In San Leandro, grammar school went K-7, junior high 8-9, and high school 10-12. So, if I had gone through the entire time I spent in school, I would have gone three years junior high and three years high school. In other words, it ended up that I went to junior high longer than I went to high school. Good grief, what 'good luck'! I met plenty of great kids there and I learned lots in my young adolescence about life in general, from elementary algebra to woodshop.

I tried out for the basketball team and got cut, that was a blow to my young ego. I made the team at Bret Harte Junior High in Hayward. I guess I was in those 'clumsy years' of being a teenager.

I was involved in honor society at Bancroft Junior High. We went to plays and visited University of California at Berkeley's campus.

Time Brings Changes

I graduated from Bancroft Junior High and moved to the school up the street, San Leandro High, where the big boys played ball and drove real hot cars with pretty girls at their side. I could hardly wait.

I always wanted to play sports in high school and I finally got my chance. The sophomore football coach, Caz Munoz, came to Bancroft and offered to help us get started by having us work out with weights and run so we could build ourselves up to be 'sophomore studs'!

Football practice began in the middle of August, and the first double-sessions lasted two weeks. I didn't realize what I was in for, but it was well worth it. As I look back, it was a wonderful, but grueling, life experience. When the double sessions ended, I lost about ten pounds of 'baby fat'. I gained more knowledge and strength, and learned more about the game and how a team played as one semi-large machine. I knew this as a little leaguer but it was reinforced even more. We had a fine season, going 7-2 in the win/loss column.

I moved up to Junior Varsity about two-thirds of the way through the season which I thought was impressive, as did my dad. The season ended with a smile.

I played sophomore and JV basketball. When I was a junior, I played JV basketball but I also played some Varsity. I missed getting my Varsity letter by two quarters, a little disappointing but what isn't in the game of life. More sports strategies entered into my playbook brain.

I played JV baseball my sophomore year. I was a pitcher in my 'younger days' but Coach Munoz never did let me try to even get into the rotation. He wanted me to play right field. He said the man with the strongest arm always played there. Who was I to argue? It just so happened, that he went to school with my dad and they were the best of friends in those 'darkened ages of school'.

I Learned To Work At An Early Age

Saturdays and summers saw me working at my dad's store, Fabric Lane. I worked for my grandfather doing odd jobs on his custom home building sites. I even worked at Reva's bakery next to my dad's store, cleaning up the tables and washing dishes. I disliked this chore even at home but a kid has to do what a kid has to do to earn extra money for that all-important auto. I cleaned racks where the pastries were displayed. I even sold a donut or two, and ate several freebies. I loved slow pastry days, they were the tastiest.

Getting Older Every Year

My junior year in high school was enjoyable. I was involved in advanced placement, scholastically; and played JV and Varsity football, basketball, and Varsity baseball.

I was in Honor Society most of the time but I was 'semi'-lazy. I did only enough to get my grades good enough to make the honor roll 'most of the time'. It also helped to get a better, lower, auto insurance rate. What is wrong with saving a buck or two? I only took some of the classes because they were required but I thought they were a waste of time. Kids think they know everything. Now I wish I had learned how to study better, i.e., read faster, concentrate harder, but what do they say about hindsight? It is as good as keeping up with yesterday!

Norah

I had a few young lady friends, dated and enjoyed their company but one miss stole my heart, Norah. She lived about ten blocks from me and attended a Catholic high school in Oakland. She played the cello beautifully and was a wonderful human being. I went 'steady' with her for almost a year before, during, while I was comatose, and after my mishap. I went to her house as often as possible without making a pest of myself. I took her to my Junior Prom where, in my eyes, she looked the best out of all the young ladies there. Her mom, Mrs. Clydesdale, is a dear woman, who helped me in our relationship.

Granddad And His Necessities

My granddad bought an older trailer and rented a site in the last cove at Wragg Canyon, Lake Berryessa, near Napa, California. He asked my dad if the family and he wanted to come up and visit the place. We went to check it out.

We liked it so much that, together, we rented the spot at Lake Berryessa. We bought our first boat, a sixteen-foot Fiberform outboard boat with a 65 horsepower Mercury motor. We met more fine people who had a water ski club, the 'Skibees', in the same cove where our trailer was located. I met another young lady, Aleine, and we became weekend ski friends. We water-skied, took out our parents' boats, and even went to the Berryessa Bowl, a dance spot where semi-well known groups came and performed. My friend, Louie, and I went to her house in Daly City and double-dated, what wonderful faded memories!

I Promise That.......

Towards the end of my junior year, I tossed my hat into the high school political arena. I ran for senior class president. A new venue in life, the last time I had run for office was in grammar school. I was elected class president for a quarter.

There was one thing I had not conquered which was the art of public speaking. I had to make a speech to try and convince my classmates that I deserved the highest office. My opponent was a neighbor who lived two blocks down the street, a doctor's son, another David. His dad was my mother's obstetrician and delivered me, small world. I practiced my speech over and over until I could have recited it backwards. My knees were shaking and I felt like I would 'up-chuck' at any moment but I <u>had</u> to go to school that day. I did attend school the day we were supposed to give that 'dreaded speech'. Up until the last minute, we were then told that they were not going to have us give our well-rehearsed election plea, thank you Lord for sparing me! I had my doubts concerning the outcome. The verdict came in: I won! I had actually won! The only thing is...I never saw a day in office, the reason being my auto accident.

The Near-Fatal Buy

My grandfather bought more property at Lake Almanor in northern California. My friend Louie and I were going travel up north to help him build his cabin, fish in the early evening and meet girls whenever we had the opportunity. What way to spend the summer! As it has been said, "The BEST LAID PLANS."

Louie and I helped my grandfather load his jeep and trailer with all the needed equipment, food and essentials necessary for our endeavor. We left in the morning on that fateful July 22. What happened that day, and the following four-plus months, prevent me from remembering the life-changing events that followed.

My mom had the presence of mind to document the events and I thank her for everything she did in those darkened days of David, July 22, 1969 and the many following months.

My Mother's Input On The Events

The initial shock of the accident and David's condition suddenly turning worse, which required immediate brain surgery, left us numb. I remember having a real physical pain in my chest and wondered if that is what is called heartache. Our daughters, Leni and Gail, aged 14 and 13 respectively, were hysterical at first, while I somewhat maintained a calmness. But as the hours slowly passed and reality came as to what was happening, both my husband Pete and I fell apart for a time. The following two and a half weeks were a nightmare for all of us, but I will never forget how our two little girls gave us the strength and faith. We adults actually leaned both physically and emotionally on their brave, strong, young shoulders.

Louie and David were traveling in David's convertible to Lake Almanor for three to four weeks of hard work and play at his grandfather's property. The accident occurred near Gridley at a particular crossroads called 'Robinson's corner' or 'Death Crossroads'. Apparently other accidents had happened at this spot. The boys were taken to Biggs-Gridley hospital for emergency care. From there, David was taken to Chico where Dr. John R. Clark, neurosurgeon at Enloe Memorial Hospital, awaited his arrival. We feel absolutely certain that Dr. Sullivan, the country doctor, was responsible for saving David's life at this point. His swift action in sending the boy to Chico where Dr. Clark was waiting happened in the nick of time.

Upon arrival at Gridley, we spent a few short moments with Louie, took his parents to a nearby motel, and rushed on to Chico, 22 miles north. David was already in surgery. At 2:45 a.m. Wednesday, we were allowed to see our son for a moment. His body was bruised and battered with lacerations and abrasions, but his head was a shock to look at. It was so swollen.

I remember asking Dr. Clark two questions: "Will he live?" And the doctor's answer was a shrug of the shoulders and a simple, "I don't know." The second question was, "How extensive was the damage?" The doctor said it was pretty extensive, but since no surgery was done in the brain stem area, only time will tell. He said Dave should regain consciousness within fifteen days.

Dr. Clark, at this point, took time to arrange for accommodations for us at the nearby Washington Motel. We slept there for three hours then went back to the hospital where phone calls had begun to come in from relatives.

Then the long vigil began and most important, the test of our strength and faith. Each of us, in our own way, had received the shock of losing or the possibility of losing a loved one and had begun to accept it. Accepting the situation is one thing but learning how to live and cope with it is very difficult. We were hurt and lost and wondered why this thing happened to us—other people perhaps, but not us.

One day soon after the accident, Pete and I saw two 'hippies' with their long, dirty hair, dissipated look and unhealthy coloring and I said, "Why didn't this thing happen to one of them instead of our son?" There was a pause, we looked at each other, and that was a changing moment for us in days to come. I felt a deep shame. Here I was playing GOD and making a judgment. Under the strain of despair I came to the realization that there must be a real meaning to this nightmare.

Four days after the accident, David required a second surgery to relieve more pressure. In the meantime, David definitely responded to his father's command and mine to squeeze our hands. Then a third and a fourth surgery came and no response whatsoever, for a long time. Infections began to set in airways starting in the respiratory tract and high temps upwards of 104.5.

We began to commute between Chico and home (approx. three hours each way) every third day and finally in the third week I stayed in Chico with Gail, and Pete returned home with Leni. We knew a decision had to be made to move Dave closer to home. With the help of Dr. Clark, the children's own pediatrician, and our family doctors, we decided to move Dave to Eden Hospital in Castro Valley. Dr. Pont agreed to take Dave on as his patient.

The doctor in Chico and I arranged for the ambulance trip to be taken on August 2. Against the ambulance company's policy, Gail and I were allowed to ride with Dave on the long trip home. Dr. Clark convinced them that we were stable and would cause no undue responsibility. All went well.

For the first time, the four of us were able to rest at home and begin to adjust to all the complications ever present of an indefinite future. This was an exceptionally difficult period.

Exhausted emotionally, I could have cared less about daily living, chores, shopping, and sewing for my daughters, which I have done continuously. It seemed as if every ounce of strength went to the boy whom I visited two or three times daily. After talking and talking some more to his unresponsive body, I would pray that somehow he was gaining strength through communications of my love and strength. No doubt my husband was doing the same thing in his own way. I cannot describe Pete's feeling or the girls. I can only try to express my own feelings and say that we all clung together in helplessness.

Daily living must go on and so it did, by giving myself a mental 'kick in the pants' every day. I sewed for my daughters and tried to do everything possible to comfort them and their dad. When I was down, they picked me up and vice-versa. So it went for weeks and weeks.

Dave's condition never changed greatly. At least there was no more cranial pressure. Either the shunt was working or Dave's brain was functioning 'normally'. To this day, we still don't know. I wonder if the doctors do.

Dave was in intensive care unit at Eden Hospital and although he was receiving excellent care, we felt it wasn't the right place for him. First of all, only Pete and I were allowed to visit, individually, and for very short periods of time. We felt that the boy needed more stimulus; a radio perhaps, definitely his sisters' voices. It seemed to us that the boy needed constant and good nursing care, not intensive care as such in an acute care facility. We had a less-than-adequate relationship with the doctor; he implied that the boy was going to expire, and this only added to the nightmare we were living.

Everything was out of perspective and we badly needed advice and help but we didn't know where to turn. Frankly, Dr. Pont gave up and wanted to be relieved of the responsibility, yet he could not give us advice as to where we should turn. We again turned to other doctors and after deliberation and a great deal of anxiety, decided to move Dave to Fairmont County Hospital. By this time, Dr. Edward Slagh, our family doctor, was caring for Dave. The day before moving Dave to Fairmont, Dr. Slagh sat with me and discussed the whole situation. An X-ray had shown a spot on his left lung that morning, which meant that a portion of his lung had collapsed. There was also pneumonia. The boy's weight had dropped from 195 to 127 lbs., making this another serious problem. There had been no change in the boy's level of consciousness. His chances of regaining consciousness were remote.

On September 16, after moving Dave to Fairmont, I went home feeling exhausted, defeated, and unable to think rationally or otherwise. I remember lying down and asking GOD to keep Dave in his care. No matter what might happen, please give him the chance to overcome the head injuries he sustained and give him the chance to overcome the problems in his lungs and chest. I prayed for the doctors and nurses to be guided in the care of their newest patient. I also prayed for the strength for myself, Pete, my two daughters, and all of our family and friends.

Another adjustment had begun, this time more dismal than ever. Our doubts about Fairmont Hospital began to lessen. Despite the old buildings and equipment, we could see that Dave was receiving excellent and constant care. I was relieved to see how the nurses looked after him. Because of his lung condition, the nurses turned his body nearly every hour. We were allowed to be with him anytime within reason, and our family members too, came often as well as Dave's dearest girlfriend, Norah. Norah was at his bedside; she held his hand and talked to him almost as much as myself. He loved her and I could almost sense that he knew she was there. She was at his side when he started awakening; it seemed she had a sixth sense about his coming back to the 'real world'.

X-rays were taken at least twice a week but never showed any improvement, either no change or worse. The abscess in the left lung grew larger and Dave's general condition worsened to the point that everyone felt certain that he would die soon. Near the beginning of November, we came the closest to giving up hope of the boy's awakening. His body was skin and bones and no matter how hard I tried, it is impossible to describe how he looked. I only thank GOD for sparing him pain.

He coughed often and the poison in his chest escaped through his trachea tube. This was the most vile-looking mucous one could imagine. It started coming up faster and more often, and after approximately three weeks, Dave's chest was nearly well and free of infection for the first time since the accident!

Could This Be?

A miracle was happening! Dave's eyes were bright and alert. His head turned as he watched the nurses go by. Something told me he was recognizing us. I knew he was starting to come back. Afraid to let my hopes soar, it seemed like something was about to burst inside of my chest. Each day began to bring a little more hope and everyone was generating excitement. He was waking up. Leni and Gail wanted to be with him every evening. We would rush to the hospital as soon as dinner was finished so we could talk and laugh with him.

On Thanksgiving Day, we asked Dave what he would like from the turkey. 'White meat'! Just like always. Another era was beginning, this time with hope for our son's recovery. The simple range of motion therapy Dave had received for months was expanded into a more involved program.

An occupational therapist began stimulation with brushes, ice, lemon, and sugar water—all with the intention of teaching him how to swallow again. It took weeks before the boy could take his first spoonful of solid food, applesauce. Up to this time he had received the food through a nasal feeding tube. A big step was made when he was finally able to eat by mouth in December. Pureed food was his diet, but it appeared that anything tasted good to him after being a finicky eater for his first seventeen years.

Onward and upward was the only way to go. Soon, the physical therapist was able to work with him on the mats, teaching him the simple process of rolling from side to side, another big step. There were ever so many challenges for Dave. He cried, cursed and became so frustrated at times that I thought the therapist would give up. These 'Angels in Blue' are capable, understanding and most important, patient.

This is where my mom's journaling stops and my story continues.

Trying To Recall

The second thing I remembered in early December was a nurse, Mrs. Grove, was taking my temperature rectally. I had to go to the bathroom, a B.M. And what does a baby do when they feel the urge to go, they let it flow, and so it did. I remember her saying, "Oh, David, David, please stop! David! Orderly, orderly!" and so it went! My first memory of this 'new life' I was about to lead.

Everyone was so excited about my awakening; they could not have been any more accommodating. It was Christmas morning and I was allowed to come home for the first of many more weekends. I was brought home in an ambulance. My folks made up our convertible couch in our den and that was where I was going to spend the entire day. I weighed about 120 lbs. and had a patch over my right eye. My trachea tube hole was more than apparent, and my clothes hung on me as if I was a little kid going through daddy's closet, trying on his clothes.

When I was thirteen, his clothes fit, and now they were much too big for this anorexic-looking young man. When I arrived at my house, the ambulance drivers took the gurney with me on it out of the vehicle and brought it to our front steps. The whole family was there to greet me. As I was taken up those stairs, and as soon as I entered the front door, our Airedale Terrier, Kelly, saw me for the first time in nearly five months. She sat up on her haunches like she was begging for food. We called it 'sitting pretty'. It was like she was saying, "Welcome back from your unconscious world and hello to your new life," and it was.

Another Time, Another Body

I weighed 195 lbs. when I had my mishap and I woke up at about 120 lbs. in the hospital. They tried to feed me baby food and Jell-O. I would have been happier with a steak, fries, and milkshake. When you haven't eaten solid food in four months and you've been tube fed for those months, your body is not the same. I looked down at my near-skeletal body and said to myself, "Who is this?" This is not how I was, what is this thing attached to my head?" I also had double vision due to the accident. I was told my right eye was swollen, black, purple, and it protruded from my face like a plum. As nature would have it, the swelling finally stopped and it shrank down to the nearly normal size after a few months. The only problem I had was a condition called 'double vision'. This is where the right eye looked out to the far right and my left eye remained in the normal position. This was just another of the 'gifts' I was given. I wore a patch over each eye, switching it every other day so that the one bad eye would strengthen itself with usage.

I awoke as a three year old mentally, in a seventeen-year-old, skinny body due to the brain matter and blood clots removed by Dr. John R. Clark, my neurosurgeon. I was a mess, but I did not realize the gravity of the situation until my mom told me what had happened. I heard what she said but it did not register. All I knew was hunger!

Hungry For Those Good Things

At about 120 lbs., I was still famished. When the nurses brought in our food for almost every meal, I would eat my portion and ask for seconds and thirds. Then, I'd see if anybody didn't finish their food, I'd eat what they had left over on their plates. I asked the orderly to bring the pay phone over so I could call my folks, tell them how bad the food was for dinner, and see if they could bring up a cheeseburger, fries and milkshake from Jerry's Drive-in. They could not refuse because I was as thin as I was in fifth grade. I held a hospital record for gaining the most weight, at that time, in one month, 31lbs. After that, I went on what I had never heard of in my entire life, a diet; more like a cut back on cheeseburgers, shakes and fries. CURSES! They tasted so good going down but they will hurt in the end. And lo and behold they weren't lying.

"Therapization"

Therapy was my life. In the beginning, I remember having a lovely black PT aide, Miss Mims. She gave me a workout in my bed, stretching my skinny body from my head to my toes, and the 'good pain' it provided. She was better than an alarm clock, stronger and friendlier. She always smiled;

it was one of her many attributes that made her one of the most delightful people I had ever met after my trauma.

Mrs. Du Val was her boss and also the head Physical Therapist at Fairmont Hospital. She was the kindest, dearest, warmest woman I had ever met other than my mom. I could talk to her at any time. She would listen to my difficulties and then we would solve them together. If anyone deserved to be a saint, she would get the nomination from me, hands down.

Mr. Hardy was my speech therapist and did his best to help retrain my brain back into the talking mode. I rolled my wheelchair down to his office every day. At first, he had me do things with my mouth. I had no idea why, except that I couldn't talk like I did before and it was frustrating. The only time I talked plainly was when I got angry at the situation before me. I didn't get mad that often but when I did, look out. My 135+ pound body which sat in a wheelchair, with a patch over one of my eyes, and unable to speak very well, got real perturbed. I blurted out in plain as can be English, what I had to get off my mind.

Hospital Pals

I made a whole group of new friends, each one different and more unique than the next. One elderly gentleman, Mr. Kavanagh, Kavie for short, worked with leather and made some of the finest purses, wallets, and belts I had ever seen.

Larry was about four feet tall and weighed nearly 75 lbs. Three of his limbs were paralyzed. He painted with his left hand and his mouth. He was an artist who accomplished more than anyone I had ever met. He had an infectious laugh that would make you want to have him giggle all the time. He was remarkable for his condition. His quick, razor-sharp mind and his great sense of humor always kept me going.

Larry, Kavie and I got in our wheelchairs and went to the cafeteria. We traveled on an uphill slope up a long covered walkway quite often during my 'stint' at Fairmont. On a few occasions, when I weighed around 150 lbs. and after I was able to, I would put on the brakes and get out of my chair. I would get behind it, grab the grips and push this four-wheeled heavy contraption up the hill. Larry always told me I had better get back in my chair before I fell down. I had no fear of falling. What else could happen to me? Heck, I had brain surgeries, was asleep forever, or so it seemed, and I still felt I was indestructible. Was I ever going to learn, someday, maybe?

Females

As I said before, I liked the girls and when the 'candy stripers' came and visited, what a treat! I remember one day a couple of them took me up to the top of C building. We looked out over the Bay Area from the San Leandro hills to the San Francisco Bay. When we were finished gazing at the sights seen from the top of the building, we got back in the elevator and were going back to my ward. The candy stripers 'took advantage of me', and we kissed. I started remembering, I liked this kissing thing.

Memories started coming back to me after a time, mostly things about my young childhood up to the time I was around eleven or twelve. I was seventeen and a half when this life-changing experience occurred, and I was almost eighteen when I awoke. Thinking back, it was as if

I could have been a shorter version of Rip Van Winkle, the only difference was, I did not 'snooze' quite as long.

And where did the years between thirteen and seventeen go? Were they gone or put on hold until further notice? Some came back in small visions of what had occurred during my young life; I called them flashbacks. They came back quickly at first then, as time progressed and like me, they slowed down, way down. I know now, that some will never return. I am extremely grateful for what I have instead of what I could have become.

Childhood

When a child first learns to walk, they explore their surroundings. They discover all the sensations put before them. I could not express myself very well orally, so I did it with one of my few remaining skills, that being my poetry. As this child, I wrote about nature and everything she, 'mother nature', encompassed.

> traveling through timber
>   the tallest trees
>   throughout the entire globe
>   more of God's little miracles
>   looking at these gigantic wonders
>   seeming to tickle the clouds
>   making them giggle so much …
>
>   they cry.

Outta Here!

I was in my hospital bed one morning and I started thinking about being in this hospital, the food was not like my mother's food. It was much worse. In my eyes, the doctors and nurses were playing a game and I was on the wrong end of the stick. I was getting the worst of it. Well darn it anyway, I was going to escape from this rotten compound. I watched how the nurses let the side rails down on my bed and said to myself, "David, you are going to escape from this horrible place and go home." I looked around and saw that no one dressed in white, 'the enemy', was in my ward, for the moment. I put my hand behind the rail and felt for the button, ah, got it. I then pushed it and the rail came down quickly, almost too fast. I thought, now is my chance.

My roommate Larry in his iron lung across the room saw what I was doing. In his raspy, whispering voice said, "You are going to fall and hurt yourself."

I said, "Larry, I have to get out of this place."

He said, "You are on your own, but if Miss Mick [the head R.N.] finds out, I don't want to be in your 'slippers.'"

So I pushed my left leg to the side of the bed and moved my right leg next to it. I used my right leg to help push my left leg over the side of the bed. As it fell off the bedside, my right leg followed it and my whole body sat upright on the side of the bed. Whoa, I don't think I like this feeling but I have to leave. Slowly I placed my good right foot on the floor and then pushed my left foot after. Then, I started to stand up, quivering like a skinny, little old man, without having the strength or balance. I tried to walk out the ward door. I took the first step with my good right foot, which could hold most of my body weight. Then came the left foot which could not, and I fell straight forward right on my face, in that most unflattering hospital gown. The orderly heard the commotion and came running in to see what it was all about.

He saw my bare behind sticking out of my hospital gown with me flat on the floor, tears in my eyes, started giggling, then between his laughter, asked what I was trying to do. And I said, "I have to get out of this hospital. It is no fun here." He picked up all 120 lbs. of me and put back in my bed. I pleaded with him not tell the head nurse, Miss Mick, what my intentions were. A few years later, I found out that he ratted me out. In other words, <u>DO NOT</u> trust your 'faithful orderly', they are required to tell someone in authority, namely, those dreaded but lovely R.N.'s. You <u>will</u> have some explaining to do, someday.

Flowing winds,
Splashing tides,
And searing sun,
Play upon our Earth;
Only to cease,
As morning approaches
Our waking eyes.

Ho! Ho! Ho!

I was fairly popular in school and my classmates wanted to give me a Christmas present I could use in my spare time. So, they were going to give me a black and white TV to help during my breaks after and between my hospital rehabilitation. They held a Blue Chip stamp book drive where they collected enough books to get a black and white TV set. But the books kept coming in, so they ended up giving me a 19" RCA color TV set and still had left over books. They turned the Blue Chip stamp books into money, in my name. Then, they gave it to the hospital for Physical Therapy equipment. That RCA color TV lasted over ten years, a great investment, but at what a price?

More Physical Therapy

I had a full schedule of therapies to do every day. I had group Physical Therapy in the mat room, at 8:30am, regular PT, then speech and occupational therapies. My tutor came to help me get the two classes I needed to graduate with my classmates. Then, more PT. Each PT session lasted half an hour. There were times I laughed and times I cried. It was extremely frustrating trying to get around the little obstacles put before me when six months prior I could have done each one with my eyes closed and one hand tied behind my back. I loved Carol Hince, my therapist. She was a little over five feet tall, barely a 100 lb. ball of fire with a ton of knowledge and experience behind her. When we first met, we almost weighed the same. I was stuck in my wheelchair, it seemed, forever. But Carol, in time, changed that. She re-taught me things I knew how to do but those 'mind changing' surgeries had removed those memories. Carol was my only touch with the real physical world. It was like I was born again, literally. It started out with learning my sensations all over. She filled my life with 'new' memories, which seemed like they were drawn from years ago. In reality, they were only done 'yesterday'.

> Winter trees look sad
> Being heavily laden
> With fresh fallen snow

I went to mat class in the early AM. I pushed myself down to the exercise room where a group of people, all with different afflictions, waited for the therapists to arrive. A man without a leg, a woman with a distorted face, stroke, a young lad on a small rolling bed, broken back, and several others 'patiently' waited. When they arrived we sat apart so that we would not bother the next person. We did not do jumping jacks or push-ups; rather, stretching was the mainstay of this group of 'crips'. When you are disabled, you have to make light of your adversity, otherwise you begin taking yourself too seriously. You could fall into a 'crippled cavern' and start feeling sorry for yourself. It is now called a 'Pity Party'. We improved day by day. I could not see it, but my body felt it as I progressed through the weeks. As time went on, I could almost see myself getting a bit stronger, more flexible and putting on a little weight (pre-diet). It was simply my 'new life'. All I could do was adjust myself accordingly and continue striving for my betterment in this wonderful life ahead of me. I did not realize what was in store. I was a '100 pounds of clay' ready to be molded into what my photograph on the wall looked like, or something similar, good luck!

After my PT mat workout, off to my feisty PT. for the first of two therapy sessions I had with Carol per day. We worked on every part of my body, from head to toe. We had a great relationship. Everything I tried to do that I accomplished, she'd share in my good feelings about the feat that happened. The exercises I did not execute correctly she'd say, we can try again, REPETITION! I needed to repeat my actions many times so that they would stick in my mind. Every move I made I had to think about before I made it, otherwise, I would either stumble or fall or a combination of both. I was a mess! I still fall on occasion, but I catch myself, now, more times than I did in the beginning. Whatever works! My skinned knees have scars on top of scars!

I watched the other patients improve and eventually leave the hospital. I guess they were not as badly injured or only had different types of dilemmas. It seems as if we all have our little burdens to bear, no matter who we are or what mind set we are in, I think all of us suffer . . . some more than others for whatever reason, "only whoever we believe in, knows for sure."

All In The Hands

I then went to occupational therapy for lessons on how to work my fingers and hands again. I was re-taught how to use my digits. Learning to brush my teeth, comb my hair, and use my eating utensils–the <u>most</u> important lessons in life. The only thing about using my fork was it was terribly heavy, everything seemed heavy, and finding the hole in my face to place it. I had a heck of a time finding it for the first 'minute or two'. When I remembered where my mouth was located and how to insert the fork, there was no stopping the 'inhalation' of food. I found out my worst, but best tasting vice in life was food. My trouble at that time was I had not eaten real food for four months or longer, even hospital food for that matter! How many people do you know crave hospital food? Not only hungry, but, I must have been a smidge 'touched'.

While I was at O.T., occupational therapy, I made a leather key case, which I still have. I cut, tooled, shaped, and punched each inch of the case. I relearned the finite ways of movement with my fingers, hands, arms, shoulders, posture, things I did not remember from days gone by. This relearning process was all new to me and I went with the flow, did what they told me. I 're-grew' in to who and what I am today. Talk about a long, never-ending process!

Can You Understand Me?

After 'dancing' with my physical therapist, then came Mr. Hardy, my speech therapist. He was a tall man with a cool way about him and he never raised his voice. I never saw him get frustrated or lose control. The worst part concerning learning to speak again was getting my tongue to do what my brain told it to do. All it wanted to do was lay there, like it was still in a coma while the rest of me was wide awake. Well my eyes were open anyway. Mr. Hardy had me re-learn the words I once knew, say them, tell me how they should be formed in my mouth. I still have that same lazy tongue and I cannot get rid of it. It got used to the sleeping mode; its owner did not.

Zzzzzzzzzzzz

Then, I had my nap time from 2-3 in the afternoon. What a relief from all the happenings during the first half of the day! I had not had enough R&R over the past four months. Most seventeen year olds are extremely active and more than ready to go out on some adventure. My adventure was my dream world, where I sometimes slept until they woke me up near dinner time. Dinners were a feast to me, but to many of my fellow patients (inmates), they were barely edible. I remembered from my younger days that I disliked broccoli, liver, and cauliflower. I guess I was a little bit picky. All right, I was a lot picky! I have grown up a little more now, but not too much of an extreme.

Hey, Teach

After awakening, I went back to the 'school of hospitalization', this time with a real schoolteacher, Olive Heckman. All I needed to graduate from high school were two classes. Mr. Williams, the San Leandro High School principal, was a great friend who understood the situation. I was accommodated in every way possible to graduate with my class. He was a fine, gentle man and I will always admire him for his assistance. He and his daughter Jane, who was in my class, came up to the hospital and visited with me. If my male friends knew that, I would have gotten the razz! Teens, both male and female, do get bitten by the green eyed envy bug. I would have traded <u>my</u> position with them any time they wanted, no takers.

Mrs. Heckman was a kind, patient woman who never belittled me but instead, continually praised and encouraged me to strive and not give up, unlike some of her other students who were in conditions comparable to mine. After reading a passage or two in the history book, she would ask me what I read, and many times I'd reply, "I don't remember." Then, when I'd forget, which was often, she'd give me clues to figure out the correct answer. Thus, it made the ol' brain work again. Have you ever tried to start an old jalopy with a nearly-dead battery? It was almost impossible, but she was the jumper cable and I, the nearly-dead battery, tried and tried and it finally kicked over and began running again. My brain ran extremely rough at first, it still runs rough, misses, sputters and stutters, yet never quite dies, much like myself. I had to do homework, even in the hospital. I read my books, over and over, studying hard for the new lesson about to come the next day. I passed the two courses I needed to graduate with my class. She was a lifesaver, helping me to re-start my brain; my study habits, the ones I had, were not that good. My improvement had only one direction to go.......up. To her, my heartfelt thanks!

Gold opalescence
Playing hide and seek behind
The clouds; shine on sun.

My P.T.-I-Zation

The physical therapist for an afternoon session was my 'personal trainer of human beings', Carol. The second time was a bit tougher for this 'old' young man. Repetition was necessary for the physical re-training process needed for what was left of my brain and the muscles below. I had to re-learn how my body once worked. I had a dropped-left-sided body from my ears to my feet. 'There was a crooked man who walked a crooked mile'. I, being the crooked man, had to deal with my newly created limitations.

Carol began working with me soon after getting into my new mode of transportation, the wheelchair. She had me attempting things I vaguely remembering doing, but then again not. I recalled the process of getting one part of the body to do the prescribed motions. I was a three year old baby in a skinny 120 lb., seventeen-year-old body. Physically, and emotionally, I was a mess! Starting over at seventeen would be a large task by anyone's standards, but if someone had to do it, might as well be me. Guess I might be considered a glutton for punishment!

There was a huge blow up ball, about 3½ feet in diameter. It was like a big beach ball that I laid upon and Carol watched my body's reactions to the various movements. She made the ball move from side to side, forward and backward. It was sometimes fun and sometimes scary. At first, I did not like falling off the ball, but as time progressed, it got to be fun, almost game-like. She tried to get my body's balance mechanisms to return. At first, they improved daily, then weekly, then monthly, and now they come whenever they feel like it. They have a mind of their own. Some days I am okay, other days I should not have even gotten out of bed but I did anyway just to keep my sanity.

I had to set goals, making myself strive to achieve. I <u>had</u> to get out of this hospital or any hospital. This is a necessary but 'un-fun' place to be where people have to stay to get over any affliction. I began making these goals a part of my daily duties.

1. I have to do everything that Carol tells me so that I will get better.

2. As I improve, more activities will come my way.

3. All my other therapists need to be treated in the same manner. It is called RESPECT, for everyone and everything they try to do to help to improve in my being. They knew plenty more than I could even think of plus they had a lot more experience.

All I knew was this: I wanted to get better so that I could improve enough to leave this 'dreaded den of rehabilitation'. I wanted to go home to mom's home cooking, her kind words of encouragement and the love of my family which I once knew. It wasn't to be! I did not discover this fact until a few months later. I was <u>not</u> the same person I once was, and my family was either going to accept me for the new David I became, or reject me, as a few of them did.

My dad, in his own way, tried to get me to improve by sometimes making me angry. My guess was he tried to motivate me to make my body more mobile. He tried it through 'his German humor'. He would ask me a question in front of friends. I responded, "I do not know the answer," so he would tell me the answer. Two minutes later he would ask me the same question, I would reply, "I don't remember," which was my usual response. Then he would get his 'jollies' by laughing at me, usually, in front of his buddies. I wanted to hit him with my fist but I could not raise my good hand quick enough; actually I did not have a good hand. All this did was frustrate me, but he couldn't see that. All that he was accomplishing was driving me farther and farther away. I loved him but I did not like him for a long time for doing this to me. I have come to realize that when a person has been in a coma for as long as I was, they tend to lose much of their ability to reason. It was as though I was another individual, almost a three-year-old child with no life experiences to fall back on for their own type of security.

One day, after I was allowed to come home on weekends, I was in my wheelchair chair, weighing in at about 125 lbs., with a patch over my bad eye. In our TV room/den, my thirteen-year-old sister approached. I always appreciated and loved her, maybe even more than my middle sister. She told me that she hated me and started to beat me up. I did not know what was going on so I put my only hand I could lift up to protect myself. I couldn't yell very loud, due to the fact that my lung capacity had been cut by almost a half from my having pneumonia for about three months during my four-plus month coma. By the grace of our creator, Mom heard what was going on and came to the room to find out what all the commotion was about. She saw my sister punching me out and she spoke in her sternest of voices, "Gail Ann, stop that right now or I will use the wooden spoon on your behind."

She did stop, but all I have to say is thank heavens for my skinny, bony right arm that protected my recently 'broken head', and for a mother with great hearing and that second gift of intuition. As I think back upon this incident, jealousy was more than likely the cause of her outbreak. She must have thought that everyone was giving me all his or her attention. She felt ignored during those formative years where everything was about her. It was so important that nothing else matters but her needs and she took her frustrations out on my skinny fragile body. It is not a lot of fun being your little sister's punching bag. Since then, we have come to terms and life is finally good for all involved.

From a chipmunk's eye view

Hoot owl sits on the edge of night
Watching the forest below
Ready to swoop upon my plight
Trying to scare me so.
Hoot owl speaks in a questioning voice
Loudly so all can hear
Asking me what is my choice
In a tone that creates fear.
The choice he gives is to live or die
As movement starts to surround him,
He flaps his wings and begins to fly,
This moment surly seems dim.
Down he comes, I hide from sight
To you my friend, I will say, 'good night'.

Sister's Love

My 'older' younger sister, Leni, whom I was not that close with during my life before my auto accident, took over being my dearest friend. She would help me whenever I was in need of assistance while at home. She was actually a pretty decent young lady to be around, although I never realized that until after my awakening. She is extremely bright, kind with never a bad word to leave her mouth unless it was a sometimes needed criticism; actually, she is a lot like her father in that way.

The 'Rock'

There was one young man, 'Rocky,' an athlete I played baseball with in 1965, my first summer baseball and Babe Ruth leagues when I was in my early teens. He was a terrific catcher for Pring's Coffee Shop, another team in our Babe Ruth league. At the time of the accident, we played for our high school team. After my awakening, he came up to Fairmont Hospital to visit me. He was always good to me and made me laugh—a wonderful stimulating concept for a young man who had lost most of what a sense of humor can do for people. He stirred up feelings of togetherness and camaraderie. Rocky used to call me a name I guess he got from the TV show, 'All in the Family', 'Meathead'. I laughed about it for the first couple of times but after a while it got a little old. Rocky helped my mom out quite a bit when Dad was not there. When I needed lifting and only Mom was around, the 'Rock' would gladly help with the necessary movement of this disabled body. And if dinnertime came upon us, Mom would always offer Rocky the opportunity of eating with our family. Naturally he did. Who wouldn't have jumped at the chance of indulging in her wonderful cooking? My mother was a great cook, beyond description. I have come to realize, I just took it for granted. She on the other hand, would always downplay her superb display of cooking abilities. My mother reminded me of the female version of Walter Brennan who once said of his skills, "No brag, just fact!"

Moe & Ellie

Two young ladies, Moe and Ellie, were my schoolmates. Ellie was a year younger than me; she was the 'clown' and she was always joking around. They came up to see me while I was hospitalized quite a bit. I enjoyed their company. One Saturday evening, after I was released from the hospital, they took me to see a movie, *Butch Cassidy and the Sundance Kid*. They used to make fun of me with my yawning and falling asleep. I could fall asleep at the drop of hat, one of the difficulties of my being brain-damaged. Before they came to pick me up, they made me promise that I would <u>NOT</u> fall asleep during the movie.

We went to the drive-in, parked our car, hung the sound box in the window, got popcorn and drinks, and the show came on. The first half hour I was fine, the next fifteen minutes my eyes started to grow heavy, and within five minutes I was gone—off to that place I had grown accustomed to for those four-plus months a little while back. When they noticed that I was off in Never-Never Land, they tugged and pulled and shoved me until I awoke. I said, "Go away, don't bother me, I'm tired," then I realized where I was and what was going on. I remembered what I had promised prior to going to the show, *I will not fall asleep, I will not fall asleep*, and what happened, I fell asleep. The movie was great from what little I could recall. When you are brain-damaged, your life changes in such a large, unimaginable way. People with 'normal brains' who have not undergone craniotomies cannot conceive. The problems and struggles can and will develop sooner or later. When they saw me asleep, did they get on my case? They said I promised that I would not fall asleep, and I did, what else could I do? I simply listened to my inner voice, that of the human body, which told me, close your eyes and snooze and I did just that, sue me! I was like a five year old in a 75-year-old body. My old man's body was slow, flabby, loose skin, uncoordinated, and it has its painful moments. It must continue to strive for the best life possible it can have under its condition. But that did not bother my friend's feelings for me, they still loved me just the same... love is good!

I Witnessed A Miracle

I was lying in my bed one morning after a long night's sleep, like I did every night. I was looking down at my 'two doorknobs' (I still had double vision from the accident), when all of a sudden, my two doorknobs started moving closer together, closer and closer, then they became one. I thought oh my goodness, I don't have double vision anymore. Wishful thinking! Then I got out of my bed, hobbled out my door to my folks' bedroom, knocked and went inside. By the time I got to my mother's side of the bed, I could feel my eyes had gone back to their 'normal' double vision state. I closed them and said wait a minute. I prayed they would go back to the normal correct position, I opened them and they both looked directly at mom. She was amazed at what she saw and began to weep tears of joy. She remembered what the eye doctor had told us several weeks prior to this event when he talked of more surgery. This time a procedure was needed to make the right eye come back to normal by cutting the muscle in the eye socket allowing the eye to move to its correct position. I was not too excited about this. Hadn't I had enough? I had to exercise my eyes whenever I thought about it. I looked at a stationary object then at another about ten feet to the right of it, then quickly back to the original object. My left eye would always move faster than my right eye because of the damage incurred during my accident. I must have looked a little strange moving my eyes back and forth without any person or thing to be seen, like the Jimmy Stewart movie, Harvey.

I have a favorite season

When everything is green
And here is the reason
So you will see what I mean.

The rain starts in October
It continues through the fall
And on into the winter
When the snow begins its call.

As the snow starts melting
There is freshness in the air
Vanishing white is such a sight
For spring is back to share.

My Return

I got to attend my high school for about the last month, only first period with Mr. Hillis. After that, my dad picked me up and we went back to my 'home away from home', to start my never-ending therapies. I did not have to go to my mat class anymore; I graduated from that in a manner of speaking. I spent the rest of the day in my 'normal' mode doing hospital duties; therapy was my life. At the time, I thought I had to be the most 'THERAPIZED' individual on planet Earth. I have come to realize I am not, only another (im)patient.

The Biggest Dance Of My Life

While I was in the hospital, Henry Guerrero, the town mortician and good friend of my father, came to visit me. We lived about five houses up the street from him. He had heard that my condition was not that good. In his generous way, told me that when and if I should be able to graduate with my class and go to the senior ball, he would let me use one of his limousines. I could take my unknown date to this upcoming happy occasion. There was a song girl, Nancy, who I always thought was pretty but I never told her. I was informed by my sister that if I asked her, she would go to the ball with me. I thought this would never happen. Reason being, I was not the same guy my friends once knew, I was a brain-damaged accident victim. I asked Nancy and she actually said yes. Oh my goodness, I have a date! We double-dated with Rocky and he took my sister, Leni. My dad got the promised limo from Hank's mortuary and brought it home. Now that was style! I wore a blue dinner jacket. It was the fanciest look I had worn in my entire life, and it felt good, now, if it will only help impress my date. I bought her a corsage from Myamura's flowers, my classmate's father's florist shop, an orchid, it was pretty but not as pretty as Nancy. Dark hair, big brown eyes and lovely, was I lucky or what? And best of all, she accepted me for who I was, not what I used to be…unlike many people who, years later, still did not want to be around me, their loss.

We arrived at her home only to be greeted by her mom at the front door. We were welcomed in and then Nancy came out from the rear of the house in a gorgeous off-white evening gown. WOW! Was I impressed! I didn't think anything could look that good! I gave her the corsage and tried to pin it on. I needed a little help, so her mom assisted me with the attaching. Boy, she looked good, I couldn't get over it. They took pictures and we said our good-byes to her parents and we walked to the limo. My 'chauffeur dad' opened the door for us, we entered and away we went to our senior ball.

We drove to the Sunol Valley Country Club where the festivities were to begin. Even Rocky appeared excited as he talked most of the way there. He was always a talker, but this brought out the 'best' in the Rock. We pulled up to the country club and Dad jumped out of the limo, almost like a real chauffeur would have in the movies. I got out, held my arm out for Nancy, she took it, arose, and out she came. Rocky and Leni followed, and in we went to our senior ball. My dad promised he would pick us up after the affair and he drove back to our house until 'his services were required'. Somewhere in what was left of my mind was a remembrance of this place. My senior ball committee and I went there to look at this as a possible site months before. We were treated wonderfully by the Sunol Club staff, who did more than I even expected. Heck, I had never been to anything quite like this, except maybe an aunt's wedding years ago. But I never had a date who looked this good to accompany me, either.

The evening was fabulous. There was fine food, great music, and an altogether memorable evening. Dad came back to pick us up. I wished he would <u>not</u> have been so prompt, but that's my dad. We drove home way too fast for my liking, but Nancy and I 'snuggled' a bit while en route as did Rocky and Leni. I appreciated that rollup window between the driver and us passengers, what a great invention!

Dad brought Nancy and me to her front drive, and we got out and started slowly walking to her front door. We turned and looked at each other; I thanked her for the wonderful time we shared and I hoped I wasn't too much of a burden having a 'crip' take her to the ball. She replied in her own gentle way of what a good time she had attending our final high school dance. We put our arms around each other, hugged, and fondly kissed good night. She was a great kisser. I returned to the limo and got in the front seat with Dad. Rocky and Leni cuddled some more. We put the dividing window up so we wouldn't have to watch their goings-on. We came home, Rocky and Leni said their good-byes, Rocky took off in his yellow '67 Mustang, and I headed to my room. I was pleasantly 'grilled' by my mother, who had to know everything about the evening. I was still excited, told her a little bit about what had occurred, yawned and said, "Ma, I need my beauty sleep (ha ha)." Off I traveled into dreamland, a most secure place, what a terrific night!

The next week brought another life-changing event, my high school graduation. Prior to my accident, I had always thought that my high school graduation would not be that big of an event. Another day in the life of…It so happened that it <u>was</u> a large accomplishment for this young man, according to some of my acquaintances, young and old. They had a special seat for me on the stage in the quad, along with the principal, vice principal, counselors and a group of other valued members of the community. They called name after name; we had a fairly large class it seemed to never end. It finally did with Mr. Williams giving me my diploma, shaking my hand and congratulating me. I could not have done this without all my tutors, teachers, friends and loving people who cared enough to give me their very best and they did.

The crying trees

A gentle rain
Softly strikes
The lucky leaves
Receiving their
Most needed moisture,
Uplifted branches
Do thank the sky.

Back To The Grind

Then came the start of summer, the best time of the year for most graduating kids. It was the time for them for final college preparations, but for me, a different story. It was a time to return to the hospital every day for more of what I called getting THERAPIZED, and 'dancing with my therapists'. I had several goals I wanted to achieve while I was an outpatient at Fairmont Hospital. My desire was to get a better sense of balance so I could use a cane while walking or standing. I wanted to return to the old David—he won't come back and never will. I know that now, but at least I tried. When one door closes another cracks open enough to get your nose inside, then you go from there. The only way to travel is down that long lonesome road.

Cycling

When I was only a young lad
And traveled on my trike
Was jealous of all those big kids
And the way each rode his bike.
But three wheels became two
In a matter of several years
When I look back upon this fact
Good grief, what wasted tears.
For now I have my ten-speed
And on it I cruise around.
The wind races past my ears
It is the best thing I have ever found.

I tried to bicycle on my three-speed Schwinn that I had for nearly ten years. I fell off, got on again, tried again, fell—the balance was not there. Only scraped knees, the beginning of what was to continually happen for the rest of my life. I had scars from my brain to my dead great left toe, no connection. A few days later, I tried another approach, my sister's 20" Schwinn banana-seat bike. It did not have the bar between the handlebars and the larger seat did not let me lose my balance while trying to get onto the bike. I got on it, started to sit on the seat, let it roll down the driveway, brought my feet up to the pedals and started to pump. What a neat sensation! I hadn't felt the wind rush through what was left of my hair since I had gone bicycling before my accident. When I felt I was going to tip over, I simply put out my feet and caught myself. What a difference! I don't like to fall down…it has to be a male thing.

A Cut Back

Back to therapy, the only thing was that my meeting with Carol everyday was cut back to three times a week, but I still enjoyed her company. How could they do this to me? She was my 'rock' that I could talk to without her telling me I was wrong or scolding me for doing a naughty thing. She was my confidante. I must have asked her to marry me a couple of times, the pupil-patient/teacher-therapist thing.

On The Road Again

It was late June and I knew if I wanted to go to school, I would have to drive again. I had a great friend, Mr. Todd, my general shop teacher back in eighth grade who taught driver's training. I hadn't lost my license to drive because of my accident. I hadn't used it in close to a year. Mr. Todd graciously offered to teach me how to drive again. I was nervous about getting behind the wheel but thought it should be like bicycling, it will all come back. It was not too hard getting into the swing of things again. I successfully completed the week-long driving course. In the early evening, Mr. Todd came to my house and had my dad and mom take a ride with me to show them how I handled the auto once more. He had the dual controls on his side so my father would not jump out of his skin. I did fine and tried to prove to my father that I was almost OK to drive. Even today, Dad would prefer to drive. Actually I'd rather ride with him—he has a fancier set of wheels.

My Second Car

My grandfather came through on his bet with me, when I was only a child. 'Granddaddy' and I bet that when I was sixteen, if I did not smoke, he would buy me a Honda motorcycle or when I turned eighteen he would buy me a car. I opted for the car at eighteen because I already had an auto that served me well. I had hoped he would buy a 1967 Pontiac GTO. That was my favorite affordable car at the time. When he came through on the bet, he drove down our street in a 1963 Kharmann Ghia. I could not show how disappointed I was about his generosity. I got in and sat down on the low seat, tried to work the pedals, clutch, brake and gas. Granddad did not realize that I had a dropped left foot. This meant I needed to pull my pants leg up to help pick up my left foot to step on the clutch and make it release the gears. Over time, I picked up my foot almost naturally without using the pick-up theory. I did not realize what he did was a favor to me by making parts of my body work a bit harder to get the results needed to become more like the average person everybody else was. Granddad was a therapist in his own way and I thank him for that.

In silent feeling
We know ourselves
Only if one listens
To what is not heard.

C-C-C-College

I knew it was time to make a big decision in my life, continue in school, college. I never went to a junior college before, but I heard a lot about the activities and how the girls abounded. So my mom and I enrolled for the summer quarter, a history class and a weight training class for me and a health class for Mom. It was like she wasn't healthy enough. I found out that college was a brand new thing, harder than I could even imagine, for an extremely 'young' high school grad. My biggest problem was that I could not remember what I read. I would sit down and read a passage from a history book and after a paragraph or two, I would ask myself what I had just read. I could not even remember the name of the book I was reading. I could think back and tell you what I got for Christmas in my fifth year as a child, but what I had just read, never mind. The brain could not grasp or retain the trials of being traumatized. The short term memories do not go together, like oil and water.

My friend from my first neighborhood, Dr. Larson, was second man on the totem pole at Chabot Junior College. My mom and I went to the college to talk to him about my enrollment at that fine institution of higher learning in the fall quarter. He knew all about my 'little' problem and did everything he could to help me get around the 'system'. He gave me a waiver to avoid taking the ACT, a college entrance exam to place you in a position of higher learning. I know for a fact that I would not have been able to pass it, leaving me in the state of limbo where I, in all probability, would still be. More than likely, I would be living at home with my folks, not a pretty picture. Dr. Larson was an extremely intelligent, good and fair human being. Whenever I had a problem or difficulty with my instructors or college staff, he was there with advice or spoke to the person with whom I had the problem. Dr. Larson was one of my guides who I will always admire and thank.

When I started college, the first fall quarter after my mishap, I took a Tutorials 100 class which included English, speech, and psychology. It was a twelve-unit large class with five instructors and a head instructor who watched over all 75 students who ranged in age from 18 to 70. Most had been out of school due to illness, the Viet Nam and Korean Wars, parenting or retirement boredom. I qualified under the 'could not handle the real school demands' since I was considered, even then, 'almost totally disabled.' I did not want to be a burden to anybody but I was—so on we go. The classes were hard for this brain-traumatized eighteen-year-old young man. My mentality was around age eight. How many eight year olds do you know that are college freshmen, who wear a 6'1" limping body, stutter and are a little confused as to their whereabouts part of the time? I only knew one and I had to live with him, lucky me! The classes were a bit more than this young man could handle, so fortunately, I took the classes under a credit/no credit basis. I finished the block of classes hoping that I passed all my courses, yet, in the back of my mind, I knew I did not pass those subjects. I did not tell my folks about my shortcoming but I thought they must have known. I was not the same young man who had dreams of becoming a football-playing orthodontist.

A Man Named Moe

Along with my academic (mis-) trials, I did get some credit, half a unit worth when I took a weight training class. In this weight room, there were football, soccer, and track athletes, 'real men' like I was going to be someday. I started to push the weights hard, but ten pounds was too heavy for me. I got winded just thinking about walking to the track, and running around it was impossible in the beginning. I did not remember who this person was inside my 'fragile corpse-like body'. The young man I thought I knew was semi-tough yet sensitive enough to know when to be gentle. It was as though I was a weak little kid starting all over again, with everything I attempted. I had to learn things most persons my age had known for a long time. It was extremely frustrating, but a kid's gotta do what a kid's gotta do, and I did it at a much slower pace. I had two speeds, slow and stop. So, I lifted light weights, very light weights, and built myself up at a snail's pace without the possibility of hurting myself 'again'. When my weight class session was almost over on the first day, Coach Wellman had us run around the track for a half a mile then come in for showers. I walked, hobbled due to my dropped left foot. I only wanted to be like everybody else. The entire class started to jog around the quarter-mile oval. I waited until the last person was heading down the track, then I jogged three steps, fell on my left knee, and tumbled headlong onto the track surface. I got up, started down the track again and again I fell on that same left knee. I looked down and saw that both knees were bleeding fairly badly and the coach noticed the same thing. He told me to go into the team room and get Moe, the athletic trainer, to tend to my legs.

Moe was a large man with a big bellowing voice, huge hands and a kind but firm caring manner about him. He washed my knees as he was speaking to me; he didn't even watch what he was doing. I guessed the reason for this was he had done his job for so long all this had become automatic. My mental state had me shed a few tears, of embarrassment mostly. While he was mending me, his joking manner had me laughing out loud before he was even done. Moe became another one of my Chabot guides, when Dr. Larson was busy, Moe was always there. Moe <u>will</u> <u>always</u> be a good friend.

Shake Your Booty

There were dances at Chabot almost every Friday night after the football games. I loved to dance; I was never very good at it, even five years did <u>not</u> make me any more coordinated than I was at thirteen. When the Lord was passing out rhythm, I must have been hiding behind a cloud. To think I played the drums in grammar school! They must have been terribly hard up for a person with no talent, a pair of drum sticks with a futile desire to be in the band. I had several experiences with the ladies at these dances. First of all, I had to work up the courage to ask the girl to dance with me. Next, was getting over the fear of her seeing me walk, I was embarrassed about my limp. How many eighteen year olds do you know who thought they had it together, but forgot where they put it? Well, I got to the young lady, as I was saying to myself, "Lord, give me strength." I then asked, "Would you like to dance?" She gave me the once over and said, "No thanks!" I thought this might happen, but I didn't expect it so soon into the evening. I went to the men's room, checked everything over, went back out and tried again. This happened several times before I got my first chance to show them what I had, which at the time I did not think was that much or that good. Finally a sweet young thing said, sure she'd like to dance. I almost passed out, she said yes, now what do I do? I stuck out my hand, she took it and to the dance floor we went. Lucky for me it was a fast song so when you dance, nothing really matters as long as you keep some eye contact with your partner and make sure you smile. You are supposed to enjoy it instead of dreading your next move. I was an all-out rookie at eighteen. As the evening and the hours dwindled into late night, my stamina was all but drained. I drove home in my 1963 Karmann Ghia with a smile on my face. I knew that I had broken 'my' post-brain-trauma idea that I was not worth anything and actually a few young ladies wanted me as a dance partner. The things in life that make you grin.

when I am

i am lonely
people say they are my friends,
but who calls me…
some call me……. names.
when I approach ……. they retreat
when I speak… they turn deaf ears to my words
or
shrug weak shoulders and walk away,
when I show them my writing…… they turn their heads.
why i am lonely…….nobody cares.

Would You Do Me The Honor

When I started to return to the dating scene, my first girlfriend came to mind, Heidi. I called her up and asked her if she would like to try again, eight years later? I wondered if she remembered what happened years ago. I did. We went miniature golfing and then out for a sundae at a soda fountain we both knew. We started to head home, came to her apartment, I got out and held the door for her, as I was accustomed to doing. She got out, took my hand and we walked to her front door. I said to myself, is she going to kiss me or am I going to go home smelling my breath and feeling bad about the evening, again? We looked at each other, took one another in our arms and kissed, a terrific sensation. I had finally found the two lips that I almost kissed many years ago. I wanted to renew this friendship but I was too afraid she might turn me down to make the second move. I guess I will always wonder what could have been.

No One

Lonely vacant heart
No one seems to care
All this love with my realm
No one wants to share.
Depressed despondent feelings
Are all kept deep inside,
Total useless friendship
I simply cannot hide.
Why can't someone see this hurt
Way down within my soul?
I wish that I could find some one
To fill this blackened hole….

My Own Dad Fired Me!

I had always worked from age twelve until seventeen, then… my mishap. My dad tried to have me work at his store again. I guess I was not worth the extra time and patience it would have taken to retrain this large un-coordinated body of a son, plus they had stairs, a lot of them. Most people fall <u>down</u> stairs, I fell <u>up</u> them. It was too difficult for me to pick up the bolts of fabric, take them to the stairs, keeping my balance and moving toward the top, especially with a dropped left foot. Impossible! I tried getting a job when you look fairly normal but have the attention span of a three year old. When your memory of things you have done in the past five minutes has been all but totally removed from your head. GOOD LUCK!

This lopsided body which I possess
makes up my exterior,
the jumbled words that come from my mouth,
why am I so inferior?
People can't see what makes up my mind
all they can see is my limp
my stuttering speech is all they hear,
I know why they think me a wimp.
I try my hardest to do my best
I only do what I can,
someday I hope someone will say
that I am truly a man.

I Finally Got Hired

The only place I could get a job at was at the hospital where I awoke and it was under a government program. This program was for disabled persons who could only make $120.00 per month and you would work four hours a day, five days a week. I went to school for the first half of the day and came back to Fairmont for the last half to finish it out. It was located in central supply where I did the grunt work. I washed the aseptoes, containers that are used to feed the patients with a liquid formula while they are unable to feed themselves. Most were paralyzed, comatose or had some other affliction. I also washed out the sterilizing units for the entire hospital. We wrapped each individual piece of equipment for hospital use, put it onto a sliding carrier, then placed it into the autoclave where it steam-cleaned the equipment for sanitation purposes leaving everything germ-proof. The unit was spotless all the time. It was almost too clean except for the mind of one of the orderlies, Mike. He was always calling one of the non-nurse persons a name, her name was Myrtle, but he always called her Myrt. Then he would go around the room saying Myrt, Myrt, like a parrot. It was rather cute at first but it got old after a short while. She never seemed to get offended. What a patient pretty little woman, more patient that I would have been.

Visiting My Home Away From Home

When I worked at Fairmont, I used to go over to C-2, my 'wake-up ward' during my break time. One day when I was on the women's side talking to one of the nurses, I noticed a new face. She was a dark-haired, brown-eyed, thin, pretty little thing with the sweetest look upon her silent face. I asked, "Who is this?" The nurse said, "Her name is Sharon, and she was in an auto accident similar to yours minus the brain surgery and she is comatose like you were, also." I knew what to do when you 'meet' a person in this state from past experience, so I started a gentle conversation with her. She did not even flinch, smile or say how are you, not that I expected her to, only wishful thinking. I did this, went to her bedside, same time, for nearly four weeks. She lay there motionless. Then, one day she seemed to smile when I gently squeezed her hand. I thought I felt her squeezing back. I did it again and I could have sworn she knew I was there. I did not tell anyone for fear of them thinking I was nuttier than usual. Two weeks later, she did start awakening. I was back at her bed talking softly and calmly, trying not to scare or make her afraid of me. In one of our conversations, she mentioned she was from Fremont; she recalled her accident and her arresting officer's name, Dan Feliciano. I was amazed and asked her to repeat that name. She did. I said that was my natural father. She told me that he was a neighbor of hers and he lived about two blocks from her house.

When Sharon got out of the hospital, I went to see her. We were only 'disabled kids' trying to have a good time with our lives. We went out one day and then she told me to pull over at this house. I did, unknowing what was going to happen. We got out of the Kharmann Ghia, went to the door and knocked. This woman, who I had never met or even seen, said, hello David, gave me a big kiss on my lips. I did not even know her, and said, please come in. We obliged, entered her home then out from the back room, a tall, handsome, auburn haired man with a ruddy complexion and resemblance to, guess who? It took me aback a little, and I said, "Darn, I think you look like me." He replied, "No, you look like me." We became instant friends. Dan Feliciano was his name. I asked him a question I had always wondered, what was his nationality? He told me he was Puerto Rican. I guessed he was Italian but wasn't sure. I was not sure I wanted to tell any of my friends about the fact that I was actually a cop's son. I wasn't ashamed of this, but as a matter of fact I was rather proud that he would put his life on the line every day to support his loving family. I never called him dad because I grew up with my father, Pete. I told him he was two-thirds my dad that would make him Dan. He laughed and said no problem. He was glad I was, at last, back with his family even if it only was part-time. When I would go to his house on occasion, he would never belittle me or play mental games. He loved me for what I was and who I was, not what I wasn't or what I never became. He actually listened to me when I had a problem, then we solved it together. I loved him for the time we shared.

Patrolman In The Night

A radio on his shoulder,
A pistol holstered by his hand,
There goes the man we admire
We know he understands.

As his city cried out
Needing his direction
He knows his place and what to do
as he cleans up its infection.

Rampant is the public
Gesturing as he goes by
A silent tear rolls down his cheek
And he is not supposed to cry.

He fights this never ending war
He knows what he is supposed to do
To help the city with its problems
Is what he did pursue.

When all seems dark and gloomy
And something gives you a fright
Be assured you will be secured
by the patrolman in the night.

Employment Possibilities

At Chabot's Veteran's Office was where my mother worked for over two years. Mary Evans, a tall, middle-aged woman who taught classes as well as being my mom's boss, started talking to me about a job possibility at the main post office in San Leandro. I checked into it and found it was another government program but it was perfect for me. It had great hours, from 5:30 to 7:30 Monday to Friday and five hours, 2 p.m. to 7p.m., on Saturday. It did not interfere with my schooling; the hours were short enough for me not to take up too much of my day. The pay was a lot more than I had ever gotten from any other job. The only thing bad about this job was it had a time limit; after you reached the age of twenty two, you were considered too old for the program and they let you go. But as life would have it, there was something brewing in the air.

Back To See My 'Hero'

I had not seen my neurosurgeon, Dr. Clark, since my accident. My parents thought it would be in my best interest to visit that dear man and show him how I have improved since I was in his presence the last time. Of course I had not been in the most talkative state, I was comatose, oops! We went to his office in Chico and I met him for the first time and I was fully awake. He was small man and had a powerful yet quiet way about him. I was impressed. We talked for a few minutes then he asked if I would mind stepping out of the room while he and my folks spoke. They talked for several minutes then they called me back into the room where we said our good-byes and headed home. It was a pleasure to finally meet this man who worked a near-miracle according to most. In my eyes, he is my superhero!

The Good Doctor's Advice

Back to reality! I wanted to find out what the doctor and my folks talked about. My ears were burning, and I knew it had to be about me, who else?

We returned to the doctor once more, going back the 175 miles to visit and hear what his suggestions for my continuing life might be. He took my folks into his office without me and I sat there a bit puzzled about the whole thing once more. They left his office with a concerned look about them. I asked what was the matter. They told me that it was in their best interest to send me off to school. I asked them where that would be. And they replied, in Hawaii at a small school called the Church College of Hawaii. I thought for a minute and said wow! And then, oh my goodness, does this mean they are going to get rid of me? We drove home, thought about the idea, and agreed that it would be in my best interest if I went. We then wrote the school asking about the requirements for entrance. They replied almost immediately to our inquiry. They sent a pamphlet about the school with details concerning the subjects taught, location, what was involved in getting admitted. The school tuition prices, lodging, food and whatever else we needed to be concerned about and an application to the school were included. We filled it out and sent it in. I was skeptical about the whole thing; the reason being, it was a 'religious' school. I was not that thrilled about religion in the first place, I never had too much to do with religion. I believed in a greater power, God and his Son and the Holy Spirit. I was never pushed into the genre by anyone too hard. But I thought it was an interesting concept, so I agreed to attend the school. It was a large decision for this young man to make, being away from my people for over four months per semester. Would I miss them? Probably, for a minute or two. The question was, would my mother and dad miss me or would they be glad I was gone and out of their hair for at least those four-plus months? I would be back for Christmas and then I would be gone for another four and half months. Could I truly handle this? I hoped so.

Getting Ready

Preparing for this long endeavor was a task but it was well worth the anticipation of going. That summer passed quickly as I worked at the post office, summer school and the completed the process of getting all my necessary clothes. You do not need that many clothes in Hawaii as I found out later. I would be on a small island in the middle of the Pacific Ocean with no buddies to call if I needed assistance or a mother to fall back on if I 'skinned my knee'. They, my parents, were truly going to cut the cord this time. I was twenty, so I guess it was about time to grow up and become the man I was supposed to be nearly two years before. I have come to realize that all of us age at a different rate due to the way we were brought up. Our parents' choices, the decisions we made on what we were going to do with our lives and the influence of the world, affected each and every one of us. In other words, I had to make new friends, friends of all shapes and sizes, colors and nationalities from every corner of the world. Hawaii is the melting pot of the U.S. I never had too much trouble making friends before my mishap and I was not going to now, I hoped.

We bought my airline tickets from our local travel agent with whom my dad always did business. It was almost nerve-wracking but still exciting, I had always gone on trips with family, never on my own, and so far away.

During the week before my departure, I said my good-byes to my family and friends, I went to each house in the area and kissed, shook hands, and hugged, the whole routine, and even wiped a few tears away, mostly mine. It seemed like everyone was sad I was leaving but they were happy for me. I knew it was in my best interest, and so did they.

The day of departure was upon me, I was ready to go out into the world with all my uneasy feelings put in my back pocket, and I was not going to let them out until I got to Honolulu's airport. My grandfather actually gave me $100.00 cash. He told me to have a great time with one of those grass-skirted girls while I was lying on the beach drinking my Mai Tai and watching the surfers do their thing on their boards. I guess he forgot that I was going to a Mormon school and Mormons do not drink alcohol. He dated a few Mormon girls in his younger days when the rules were even stricter. They called my flight number and it was time for me to go, off to the sandy beaches and little grass shacks. My flight was long but the stewardesses were wonderful and very helpful; I still liked the girls.

Hot And Humid

When we landed in Honolulu, there was supposed to be a school bus waiting for all the arriving students. I looked all around for a yellow bus or any other color bus; there were none to be seen. I became a bit concerned so I thought maybe I could take a cab, the school couldn't be that far away. I signaled to a cab and one promptly came over. I introduced myself told him where I wanted to go. He said his name was Peter and had to take another fare to a hotel but he would drop me off at his father's club. I could swim and take it easy for an hour or two and he would come back and drive me the rest of the way to the college. I was glad this happened because I was wearing a polyester suit and it was hot and muggy on the island. I was told that the weather is totally different in Hawaii, and when the first warm gust of hot moist air hit me right in my face when I was getting off the jet, it occurred to me that they were not kidding. We went into the club, my cab driver, Peter, told the attendants to take good care of me. They showed me the way to the locker room where I changed into my swim suit and went poolside. I took a look at the people around the pool; they were not the "normal" 'white Americans' I was used to seeing. They were mostly tanned, smaller versions of the people I was used to seeing, working in hospitals, restaurants, back home. Not like the majority of folk that I would expect to see in those types of jobs; that was my first clue that things are different over on this side of the Pacific. I should have realized this when the cab driver, Peter and a doctor's son, who brought me here, was Polynesian. He was exceptionally intelligent, and told me later this was only a summer job. He was only doing this until medical school started in the fall. I stuck my toe into the water, testing the warmth of the water. I am a coward when it comes to entering water like that.

I Reflected Back Upon

Years ago, when I was fishing in Puntzi Lake, in British Columbia with Eirwin and Thelma, my granddad's first wife, I tripped and fell out of the boat into the icy cold lake water with the two fishing poles. When I came out of the water, my entire body looked like a red humanoid with blotches of white welts on my skin the size of grapefruits. I almost scared myself. As I fell, I guess I threw the poles up into the air in order to catch my balance. But as luck would have it, so went my granddad's poles, which were worth over $1000.00. He let me know about that, immediately, after they pulled me back into the boat. As I was sitting there shaking like an epileptic having a seizure. (By the way, later in my life, I did have my share of those episodes). I noticed that a line from one of the rods had gotten hung up on the inside of the boat, I thought, could this be my life saver. Well, it just so happened that when I started pulling on that line, I pulled and pulled and at the end of that line was my granddad's fishing pole. To our surprise, the other fishing line was hooked onto that fishing reel. I pulled and pulled on that line until the other rod and reel surfaced. What a break! I know if I had lost his 'precious rods and reels', he more than likely would have disowned me. Then they would have made me pack my gear and walk home, about 1500 miles, so much for people and their 'things'.

Dip Time

Back to my swimming adventure, the pool temperature was perfect. Then I walked down the stairs to enter. When you are brain traumatized, you engulf yourself gently, feet first. It is easier on the cranium and it does not disrupt that mental organ inside. The pool water was the same temperature as the outside air so it caused no problem. I swam a little, as well as I could swim. If you think it is funny watching a little kid learn how to swim, a brain trauma victim is even more so.

I drank more pool water than I needed to and it was ocean water which can choke you just thinking about it.

Off To School, Good Grief!

I looked at the clock and noticed I had better get a move on so I wouldn't make my cab driver late for his next fare. Back at the locker room, I showered, dressed, and went out to the club lobby to wait for my driver. He pulled up and I hopped into his cab and off we went, college bound. We drove to the school, a very pretty campus. The view from the street had all palm trees and lots of two-story white buildings with brownish/red tile roofs. I was getting nervous and excited both.

Now that I am here, where do I go? What's next for me? We drove into a parking lot of this facility, stopped and asked the first person I saw where do first-time students go for housing, enrollment, food and all that other good stuff? He directed me to a building across a huge lawn area near a grove of palm trees. I went there and found a tall thin man wearing glasses and had a small mustache. He talked with a funny accent, English like. I had heard accents like that when we visited Canada but not in the USA. He helped me with my luggage. We went to the office of the dorm overseers, Mom and Pop Smiler. They registered me and then took me to men's dorm 2, #217 upstairs, room #7, which I later realized was right next to the community bathroom. There, two apartments of sixteen young men shared three toilets, four sinks and three showers. That was all well and fine, I did not mind cohabitating. I had never done it before but I was game for anything. I was about fifteen mentally, younger than I looked. This apartment had seven other beds in it. Each unit had a bed, closet, desk, small shelves and a fluorescent light above my desk at the end of my small single bed.

On the other side of this petite room was my closet, with four small drawers inside the closet, a two by two foot space for whatever I wanted to put on it—items like my change, comb, wallet, handkerchief, and all my 'male junk'. There was also about a three-and-a-half-foot-wide closet which was almost big enough to put three shirts, two pair of pants, and one pair of dress shoes, and a pair of sandals.

The room was approximately eight feet wide, twelve feet long, and ten feet high with an A-frame type ceiling. This was because I was on the top floor. The walls of each room were partitioned by closets and small dressers. The wall next to my bed had 'noisy' toilets, showers and sinks, like nothing that I had at home. Because of the vaulted ceiling, we were on the second floor and the rain had to go somewhere besides the floor of our dorm room. The floor was tiled like my old grammar school floor, even the same color, a little behind the times.

My Roommates

There were several young men already in the room. One was a Tahitian; he was short in stature but extremely fit. He looked like a Polynesian athlete/warrior, and it turned out that he was. Ben, as I was introduced, was a 'soccer stud'. He was quiet, not as aggressive as most athletes, bright, and intense in everything he did. He was a karate brown belt when we first met. In the second semester, I watched him become a black belt in karate. I would hate to meet him on a dark and lonely street. He assisted me when I needed help, made fun of me when I deserved it, and overall, was a most enjoyable young man to have as a friend.

A Tongan youth named Fonua was another roommate. He was soft-spoken yet strong. He appeared to have a purpose in this world but like most teenagers, he was still in search of that purpose.

Kam and Greg were two Chinese young men who came to this fine institution to sprout their wings. Greg was a taller than I expected of most Orientals and he was thin. He was so thin that when you turned him sideways he was hard to find, sorry Greg. He was very intelligent, a bit bashful, but he still had plenty of room to grow.

Kam, on the other hand, was, as the semester passed, was very extroverted. What surprised me the most was his English. He spoke my native tongue better than I, with perfect diction. It was incredible for a non-English speaker to grasp the language so quickly, though at times he did ask me a few questions concerning the phrases with which he was not familiar. I tried to help in my limited capacity and it worked most of the time. He became well-versed over the months we were together, I was impressed!

Richard was from New Zealand. He was not talkative and seemed to be in his own world. He had a lady friend who he was with most of the time, except when he slept.

Bob, as we called him, was known as Ichiro (meaning first-born) in his country of Japan. He was a little older than most of us by about two or three years. He was not a lot older, but enough to make us behave a little more than we were accustomed, being out on our own for the first time. He was in 'love' with an attractive haole (white) girl most of the time while he attended school.

Then there was Maxwell, a handsome six-footer with brown hair and brown eyes. He was an Australian Latter-Day Saints (L.D.S) missionary returned from Tahiti. He had the coolest, most calming voice I had ever heard in my entire life. When he said "good-day mate," he meant it. He was like the big brother I never had, but always wanted. Maxwell told me he wanted to be a radio announcer, a D.J., perfect employment for this smooth tongued Aussie. Maxwell worked at the Polynesian Cultural Center, PCC for short. He told us whenever we wanted to visit, all the students could always get in free, "no problem man."

The PCC was owned and run by the college. Most of the help for the shows that the PCC produced had college kids as the entertainers, concession help, ticket sales, and maintenance. Those shows that the PCC put on were a fabulous mixture of all the Polynesian islands. Each one demonstrated how their natives danced, prepared food and lived in harmony with each other. Though, as I later learned, the Tongans and Samoans have been at odds with each other for centuries.

While attending Church College of Hawaii, I met many people of all races, colors, and nations. Each had fascinating tales: from prejudice to pride and from parental neglect to students without parents. There were even a few students without faith to young men who went on their missions. I must say, everyone has choices in life, either good ones or poor ones, but the decision to follow whatever choice you make is yours and yours alone.

The first semester at C.C.H. was a test to see how I would do in school away from home. I did not do as well as I should have; there were too many attractive things in pretty grass skirts, you know what I mean? Even being a brain-traumatized young man, I still had desires and wants, some of which I knew I might never be able to achieve, yet I still tried. If you don't try, you will never know whether or not it was possible. So I tried everything. I watched a Tongan climb a palm tree, chopping down several coconuts with his machete. I watched the nuts fall, him husking the nut, cutting off the top end of it, drinking the milk. Then he cut the meat out of the nut, and ate the fresh coconut meat.

I also went snorkeling with a schoolmate who lived near the campus. I swam with him in the deep blue Pacific with a snorkel, mask and fins. That was a fabulous part of my journey, observing a whole new world under the sea. It was a quiet, yet busy part of life that unaware city dwellers do not even know exists.

The semester came to an end much too quickly as I look back upon it now. My grades were not the best as I had gotten in years past but they were good enough to let me return to school without being kicked out for not applying myself to the curriculum. School is hard for almost everybody; you don't have to be brain damaged to know that.

A Short Two Weeks

I prepared to come home for a two-week Christmas break with all my trinkets and little things that you would never find on the mainland. My Christmas gift was my plane fare, coming home, back to Mom's cooking, and also enjoying the love that we shared, driving my car to see friends, and simply being home again with family. The two weeks flew by, almost faster than the jet trip home from Hawaii. Before I knew it, I was on the plane back to the islands. When I was in junior high and high school, time seemed to drag and drag, then the 'real world' came into focus and it was a bit much. This accident did a number on my life, but I could deal, what choice did I have?

Maxwell picked me up at Hawaii International Airport and we were back at C.C.H. in an hour or so. He wanted to know about my family, the trip and all that good stuff. I related my story concerning what happened over the holidays. Poor Maxwell had to stay on that boring, desolate, Hawaiian island the entire duration, he and all of his lady friends. What a tragedy, while this 'crazy haole' 'suffered' through Mom's home cooking, a warm comfortable bed and a loving family. Home is good! But I knew I had to return to my school, C.C.H., for the remainder of the school year to prove myself. I needed to show this society that I was okay enough to go out into the 'real' world on my own and be ME. I started back to the Polynesian style of 'taking life a little bit slower' way of living. I did not mind it at all, as a matter of fact, I have two speeds, slow and stop unless you make me angry, then watch out! But I seldom get mad.

> Sparks of great passion
> Burst within my heart, as your
> Love came into mine

Polynesian Passion

There was a haole girl I took a fancy to; she had the prettiest green eyes, dimples, was petite and very cute. I did not fall head over heels for her, but she caught my attention in a big way. I was taken by her style, intelligence, and the way she presented herself, extremely mature for someone that young, nineteen. We introduced ourselves (her name was Mary), exchanged pleasantries, did the usual youth thing by checking each other out, mentally, socially, and physically. No hanky-panky of course. Naturally, one of the first things I told her was why I limped. I never liked to hide my affliction, I simply let people know. To me it was too obvious and I thought everyone would talk about me. I must not play those silly games, where if I pretend not to notice, maybe nobody else will and it will go away, I will get better—life does not work that way!

We became friends over the course of the semester and I invited her to the Aloha Ball, the biggest dance of the entire year. We dressed up to the nines, real fancy. I bought her an orchid corsage, and I met at her dorm and escorted her to the dance. We had a great time, wiggling our torsos around the floor, dancing, drinking the punch, and eating the Polynesian snacks. She was a fine dancer and she hugged me tightly as we glided along the floor. She glided; I faked it a little, my only way of getting through the night without making a complete fool of myself. It worked! The end of the night was approaching and was getting ready for our first good-night kiss. We got to her dorm. I was real nervous again. I thought about the Heidi experience before I even started to make 'my move'. I let go of her hand, told her what a wonderful time I had, this time I kept my eyes open, and puckered up for that evening ending kiss. What did I get? She stuck out her hand and said thanks a lot. I wanted to take her in my arms and give her something she would never forget, nor would I. It never happened! I checked my breath, it was okay. I did not have anything stuck in my teeth. It was as if I had been at this place before in a previous time in my short life. It was like the second time around. Would I ever grow up? I felt like Peter Pan, only a bigger version.

On becoming friends

A peck is just a token
Of friendship and the like
Means nothing more than 'I care'
Don't tell me to take a hike.

Our lips upon their meeting
To me is still a dream
I surely know this feeling
For us will be supreme.

Sparks will fly and flames become
And how emotions grow,
Should I ever get the chance,
My love for you I will show.

Again I walked home, back to my dorm, across the
tennis courts, under the palm trees and into my 'tiny' room.
I don't understand why some of these things happen to me,
they just do. I guess it is called life's little lessons.

Distant Days

At a time when I was younger,
Seems not too long ago
Girls were fair, I had my share,
Now there is nothing left to show.

I ponder through this channeled mind
Not trying to deceive my self
Wanting to see what just couldn't be,
As I stand alone on my shelf.

Needing someone to call my own
I thought you were my cure,
Yet you have gone and life goes on
I force myself to endure.

Time brings changes and life rearranges
Courage is what I lack,
How I long for distant days,
I wish I could bring them back.

Visiting Relations

My mom and dad came to visit me at school for a week, near the end of my stay at C.C.H. I was their tour guide, showing them the PCC and seeing some of the best Polynesian entertainment around. I introduced them to my mates at school, and they took one of my male friends, Kim, to the Kuilima Hotel for a dinner. My Tongan mate, Sione, climbed to the top of a palm tree, barefooted, chopped down more coconuts, husked them, cut them open, dug out the delicious moist meat, and shared it with them. What a treat! My folks enjoyed the atmosphere and they let me know with their smiles. It was a sad farewell when their time in Hawaii was up. I knew it would only be for a few short weeks and then I would return to the smell of that home cooking coming from Mom's kitchen. Nothing can take the place of Mom. I did not realize this until I was out and on my own for the first time, 2500 miles away is a long way to test anyone. It was worth it in the end for I came home more mature, at least I thought so! I was more comfortable with myself and I felt more at ease with people around me.

They Are Gone, For A While

Back to the grind without Mom, Dad and the good feelings we shared. School was nearly over and I needed to pass my anatomy class so I would stay above "C" level. I stayed another week to make up several tests I had taken during the term but had not done that well. I finished them up and passed the course. I liked Hawaii, but I also liked being home, home, maybe a little more, lifelong friends are a blessing.

Homeward Bound

The trip back was uneventful except for the excitement of returning to my family and friends. Even the stewardesses did not excite me that much, which was not like me. I suppose I only wanted to get back into the mainland routine, I guess I actually missed the excitement! The Hawaiian tan I got while on the island faded quickly after my return, so much for looking good at twenty-one. My dad promised me when I was in my early teens that Mom and he would take me to Reno for my twenty-first birthday. I turned twenty-one in the islands. I could actually gamble, legally, though I never tried to gamble illegally. It was my turn to beat the odds, make my mint at the slots! I found out that life is not what the commercials on the television portray. I brought up $150.00 and came home with $25.00. I never lost that much money, ever, in my young adulthood. So much for gambling, for now anyway.

My Favorite Professor

I returned to my junior college, Chabot, to finish my sophomore year. I took English 1B to help further my education. When I had previously attended Chabot, I had heard that the instructor, Mr. Rhinehart, was a great teacher. I wanted to find out for myself, so I enrolled. I had seen him playing basketball in the gym over the past quarters but I never met the man. He was a good-looking man with silvered hair, blue eyes, about six feet tall, with a well-muscled body for a middle aged man. He was late for the first day of class and I thought there must have been heavy traffic or something like that. I told Jim, as he asked to be called when my name came up for roll call, that I had heard that he could juggle, but I did not believe it. Well, he reached into his pocket and pulled out three balls. He then started to toss the balls up in the air one after the other making them go crisscross and around in a circle. Then he took out another ball, then, there were four balls up into the air. I believed it: he could juggle! After class, I told him a little about myself, the accident, etc., and that I was a poet and recited one of my many verses. He told me that was fantastic and that if I wouldn't mind, could I recite or read one every day before class began? What a silly question! Of course I responded with a "definitely." This was my chance to get out of my little self-inflicted rut, and by using my poetry, make a few friends, oh boy! The following class started with one of the poems I liked. Actually, I liked them all, but, then again, I am the poet.

It went on from there. One day after class, Jim called me to his desk and in one if his sternest, deepest voices 'commanded' me to write a poem about Women's Liberation. I thought, "You want me to write a poem on Women's Lib?" I could reason out a verse on the changing weather or a political satire, but Women's Lib? This was in the early Seventies, when the liberation of the fairer sex was in its youth. So, I wrote On Women's Lib. I suppose Jim wanted to hear my opinion on that touchy subject. The next day, I brought it to class, got up at the usual time. Before Jim came, I recited it and prayed it would not start any new wars. After I spoke my piece, actually it was Jim's idea and direction, with me as his mouthpiece. I received an ovation I could hardly believe, but it was, as I guessed, the males stood up, clapped, and cheered while the females gave me a courtesy nod of their heads. A few women put their hands together as a favor to my hard work. Those were the olden days; how much life has changed, for the better I might add.

On Women's Lib

Endless struggle …
　For what ……
　　Manhood?
　　　Reaching out in search for equality…
　　　　Unable to find…
　　　　　Yet still, women want to be treated like men.
Why I ask? You've got it good, being waited on hand and foot.
How many of you ladies would open the door for your date?
　　　Or pay the cost of a show?
　　　Or even go Dutch treat on anything?
　　Sure I'd grant you equal pay for equal work
　　But you have to show me the work first,
Even the Bible states very clearly that you came from Adam's rib
　And were put on this earth to be man's companion
　　　You may be number two
　　　But make man believe you try harder,
　　　　For then he will understand.

I wrote this under complete pressure of my friends, teachers and co-poets and it is not how I feel at this or any time after. We all have our place, whether it is behind the wheel of a diesel truck or a skillet on a stove; everything in its place and a place for everything.

david m. seymon

I Am On My Way To Bigger Things

I graduated from Chabot Junior College after 4½ years of completing my two-year undergraduate studies and was now a junior. I started to look for employment, showing off my new diploma from an institute of semi-higher learning. I hoped this would impress everyone. The only people it made a difference to were my family, some never thought I would get as far as I did, and a few of them were not that impressed. I have come to the realization that we are not supposed to impress anyone; all we need to do is feel good about ourselves. We do not need to boast about our accomplishments, only show by our actions. I went back to my old high school and talked to my friend the principal, Mr. Williams, and told him of my dilemma. He must have spoken with some higher-ups and they developed a new position at the institution. I was hired as an athletic trainer for the sports programs for all the teams. What a great thing to do for someone as low on 'the important things to do for people' list. I knew I was very fortunate to have someone like that man be a part of my life. I started in January as an athletic trainer, right in the middle of basketball season, with an old coach/friend, Mr. Garcia. He guided me through the job, what I needed to do, from passing out towels to the all wet showered young men to taping appendages on the team players. It took me awhile to get everything ingrained inside my head, but it worked for some time.

The Big School On The Hill

I started at Cal-State Hayward taking a health-related class. I was there about two weeks then my brain started to function improperly. I knew something was drastically wrong, but I could not tell anyone because my head could not think straight enough to say what was going on.

Then, the event occurred. I presume I had taken on too much.

I was informed later by my mom that about a week prior to my episode, I was doing things which were not "normal" for a person my age. Even I noticed that when

I tried to talk, I seemed to speak in garble. I would ask what I thought was normal question, and the person I was speaking with would look at me like I was from Mars. Then I was asked I to repeat the question, and I finally got it out. I thought to myself, what is wrong with this picture? I did not realize that a brain-traumatized person could only handle so much without something going wrong. Nobody told me that this might happen, and then it did. My bodily functions, walking, talking, driving, and making sense of what people were talking about were not normal. I could neither make rhyme nor reason about what I was doing with anything; it was extremely confusing. Especially at work, my co-workers were putting up with me but even they knew something was simply not right. I found out later that my involvement, according to one of my doctors, with my new job at SLHS, upper class schooling at Cal-State University, Hayward, taking a sports medicine class, and involvement in my church became too much. It was too much stress for this brain-damaged young man to endure.

I was at home sitting on a recliner in our den when suddenly the room started spinning, my throat began to close up, and I passed out. My mom fortunately heard this unusual sound, which was not what she was normally used to hearing. She came into the room and saw my body shaking and convulsing. Thank the Lord, she had taken a health class at Chabot College and recognized that I was having a Gran-Mal seizure. She knocked the chair over, I fell onto my side/stomach, she then ran to the phone, called 911, and the paramedics were there within minutes. They took me to Memorial Hospital, a couple of miles away. The next thing I knew, I had a nurse with only nubs for fingers at my bedside. I did not think this was a dream, only another day in the life of a brain-traumatized kid. They started to give me this medicine called Dilantin, an anti-convulsing drug to control seizures. This medicine was one of the reasons I appeared not all together, a little tipsy. I didn't do it on purpose, it is just the way the drug affected me. I was in Memorial Hospital for several days taking test after test, trying to figure out what was wrong with me. It had been over five years since my mind-altering brain surgeries. Normally when seizures happen, it is within the first weeks to two years or longer. It is great to be 'unique'; I guess I wear it well. After recuperating from this setback, I returned to my high school employment and back to the norm. Although nothing is normal after brain surgery!

Seizure

This funny feeling held my mind, while
A strange commotion swept my brain.
My face must have looked like I just ate a lemon
as my arm started to bounce.
I pushed the button that called for the nurse,
She didn't come, I couldn't curse.
I got out of bed and limped to the door
A nurse named Carol was walking toward me.
She asked if all was well. I could not answer
Impossible it was, I tried, couldn't she tell?
Then she saw the look on my face
and all the frustration within.
I was told to make an about face
and went back to my room.
I laid my body upon my bed, face down
So I wouldn't swallow my tongue.
I laid there forever or so it seemed,
I thought I was left for dead.
Back she came with needle in hand
Carefully she placed it below my belt.

Of course you know I got it in the end.
Gradually this trauma's finish was in sight.
My eyes grew heavy, these odd movements ceased,
To end all this, I lay in peace.

Back To Walking, Or Is There Another Way?

About a week a later, I received in the mail a notice from
the State of California that they wanted my driver's license
back, immediately. I did not understand until I was told
that once a person has lost the ability to stay conscious, the
DMV revokes their driver's license for one year. They said
that when the year passes and when I can prove to the DMV
that I am stable by having a doctor's statement, they will
reinstate my driver's license. If I should ever have another
seizure, they will take my driver's license away and never
give it back to me for the rest of my life. Oh my goodness!
What a predicament this puts me in! I found out much later
that my doctor never did report my seizures to the DMV,
thanks doc. I realized that it was all for the best that he did
not. I haven't had a seizure in thirty-six years. I'm okay. The
whole world has gone haywire.

The endless journey
Through my indescribable brain
All these incredible moments, left,
Scarring the inside of my skull.
Some of these, pleasant thoughts
Of love gone by.... Others,
Harsh visions of bad times,
all these memories hold my mind,
steadfastly against the rain.

Now, I will have to ride my bicycle, walk, or take a bus to work, every day. I chose to ride my trustworthy yellow Schwinn ten speed, come rain or shine. My bicycle and I got to the gymnasium office and went in the back door. I parked it in the supply section where not that many people enter, until the end of the day. I then put on my trainer's clothes, blue shorts, a white short- sleeve shirt and my coach's shoes. I went to my newly-formed office in the medical room, right next to the boys' locker room. It had an old teacher's desk with empty drawers waiting for all my scissors, tape, ice and hot packs, Ace bandages and the necessary equipment needed to accommodate a good trainer's office. It also had a small one-person whirlpool, sink, supply cabinets, a scale, and a massage table where all my 'victims' to be would bare most everything they had. They did, from their visible wounds to some of their most intimate feelings, mainly regarding the problems with the opposite sex. I felt a lot like a parent, Dear Abby, big brother, or combination of all three. Many were insecure as to how to speak and find out how to befriend a young lady without trying to act too cool, overbearing or smug. It made me feel like I was doing something that was actually helping these fellow young men and women. I was only 23 years old but I had several unique life experiences under my belt that aided in many situations. I helped most involved, my sharing and their receiving, then watching the results of those ideas. They also enjoyed the 'old time' stories I relayed to them when I played ball in the 'olden days'. Five years ago is a long time to these 'young studs'. Many of the male athletes had brothers who played under our same head coach. We shared the same life problems only different wine, women, and song. Actually, the wine was the same brand, Ripple. I never had a big brother only a strong Mom and Dad to help get me through my own troubled waters. They advised me in the best solutions for most of my problems. Sometimes I listened and sometimes I didn't. There were times when I wished I had paid more attention to their words. Life is the GREAT teacher; too bad many of the students were either dozing or goofing off, ah, such is life! As the old saying goes, "Life is what happens to you while you are making other plans."

Tennis Anyone?

Along with my athletic training activities, I also took care of the tennis classes, equipment, and the tennis machine, the Lob-ster.

This machine was cannon-like with a barrel and rectangular box that held the tennis balls below. The balls would be brought up one at a time to the barrel. The force of the vacuum would shoot the balls out at various speed levels and directions.

I would set the Lob-ster machine up so that it would not serve the balls too hard for the young ladies and would help them learn the correct way to hit the ball. Sometimes I would 'have' to help them stand in the proper position, striking the ball with the exact power, angle and direction to get the ball over the net and land in the right part of the court. Some, I had to help even more than others. I felt it was in the best interest of all involved to get it down correctly so they would not be made to look like the 'court fool'. While being the tennis 'semi-pro', I met one of the sweetest dark haired, blue eyed young ladies on the courts. Her name was Carol and we talked. I was always up front with every young lady I met so I told her about my disability. I hate that word, it was true, but a fact I had to admit. She, in return, told me a little about her past, men and how they treated her, both good and bad. We played a few games of tennis, used the Lob-ster machine, and enjoyed each other's company. Our fondness for each other grew, and after we had dated for about three months, she asked me to escort her to her Senior Ball. I was flattered, but I was confused a bit. I was not sure how or if a teacher/trainer/friend was supposed to get involved with the students other than on a professional basis. I was unable to drive at that time, since the state took away my driver's license for that dreaded year. Wherever we went out, Carol was always there to pick me up in her Mustang. I was embarrassed at first, but I got over it quickly enough to not let it bother me. We went to Bay-O-Vista swim club for a family party. I took her to the Blue Dolphin on the San Francisco Bay, dancing and dinner. My accident never got in the way of our relationship. She was a pleasant, wonderful way to get back into the dating scene, and I thank her for that.

Little Ms. blue eyes

I met a little miss one day
And then to my surprise
A feeling came all over me
It had to be her eyes.
Her eyes did share the color
with the sky's first morning blue
and how I that she might be
a friend who would be true.
Indeed she has been good to me
And in her special way
Having her close to me
Is how I hope she will stay.

Your Kids Get The Worst Of It

The worst thing that could ever happen, in my eyes, my mom and dad were getting a.......................... DIVORCE.

My mom came up to my room one morning and dropped this on me. I asked her why? I thought this would never happen in our family, it happened once and I thought that once was enough. I also blamed myself for their disillusionment. Who else could it have been? My accident must have been the cause. Was it my costing the family over $50,000.00+ for my wreck the reason, especially because much of it was out of my dad's own pocket? It had to have been. I wished I had never been born. I wanted to die. I even thought of committing the worst thing possible, suicide. That idea had <u>never</u> crossed my mind in my entire life until now.

Well, they actually did it, another divorce in the record books of Alameda County, California. Marriages gone south, my mom moved to an apartment on the hill. It was located above the hospital where I awoke after my accident. My dad bought a townhouse near one of my young girl friends, Geneva, had lived when I was in high school. It did not seem like it was a real-life situation, it was more like a bad dream. In my own brain-traumatized mind, I did not understand why they would do this. Dad always brought home his paycheck and paid the family bills. With what was left, they saved; we had a good life, why did they do that to the family? I thought their lives were as good as most anyone.

The love of life,
I, In need of this, will search for
'til I encounter.

Keep Movin' On

I finally left home, in a manner of speaking. I moved from my warm comfortable bedroom on Lee Avenue to a one-bedroom apartment, with central heating, in a thirteen-unit complex. It was four miles from my Lee Avenue home that my dad's family owned for many years. It was a big change! The only good thing was my grandmother on my mother's side, Thelma, and Bud, her husband, were the apartment managers for the complex. I still had some family nearby. Moving was a big step in my little life. It was the first time I was out on my own since my going to Hawaii. It was different; I had to learn how to cook, clean, do my own laundry, no Mom any more to 'pamper me'. I did not know how the real world survived without 'the MOM' nearby. I learned quickly enough, though. I traveled back and forth to my job at SLHS, into town to get haircuts, groceries and see friends. I rode my Schwinn bicycle, my only mode of travel for a year, possibly longer, without any seizures. I went to the doctor's office every week to have my Dilantin level checked. I got so used to the procedure that, by the time the nurse arrived to put the needle into my arm, I had already tied the rubber hose around my arm. I squeezed my fist to elevate the vein, getting it ready to have the needle puncture the surface of my skin. I felt like a 'clean addict'. The nurse then drew blood from my usual left arm into a tube where the red liquid was taken. Then the blood was put into a plastic bag and dropped into a group of other bags, and sent off to the laboratory. The laboratory gave the answer to the all-important question, is my level okay? Varying every week, it took about ten months for my tests to come back with the right answer. I felt like a pincushion and eventually it was at the right level. That level hardly ever stayed the same for more than a week or two, it seemed like it depended on the mental and physical pressures I had during the week. If levels were within the therapeutic range, I had nothing to worry about except getting my driver's license back, someday, maybe?

My Weekends Included

I attended the L.D.S. (Mormon) church in which I was baptized in Hawaii, riding my yellow Schwinn, every Sunday. It was a bit of a struggle to get on my bike, rack my holy books, keeping the grease from getting on my church pants from the bike chain. I did it with my 'not-so-good' sense of balance. Then, I would start to slowly pedal down my court driveway out into the real world. I got to church, listened to the sermon and talked to plenty of fine folk. I came out with a good feeling about the week to come, knowing that it was not completely in my hands, but our Creator's. When church let out, I found my way to the door, walked over to my trusty mode, unlocked it, and rode on down to the Hick'ry Pit, a fabulous restaurant in town where Dad and I met most every Sunday for our brunch. We talked about the past week's events. We had some good discussions concerning our lives, work, Dad's and my new lady friends. I did not have a lot to talk about because I usually had trouble getting a date. How do you go about finding a lady friend to go out with when, 1) you are unable to drive, 2) you do not speak very clearly, 3) you walk with an obvious limp. Who would want to even start a relationship with me? So I stayed home most of the time after work; that ol' RCA TV and I became the best of pals. A BORING LIFE I LED! I had to do something to keep myself from going totally 'insan-er', I was 'partially' there. So I tried several venues to make myself content.

My grandmother, Thelma, asked if I would like to have dinner with them. I said, "That sounds great." We ate her fine mid-west home cooking, which included beans and cornbread, stews, to venison given to us from our neighbor and tenant from across the court. What a treat! Then, a couple of months later, she dropped the bombshell on me, they were going to start charging me for all the 'extra' food she had to buy. I thought what in the world is wrong here? Does a chicken leg, extra potato, and spoonful of vegetables, validate $20.00 a week? That was approximately a quarter of my entire paycheck, plus $125.00 for rent. Was I wrong in my thinking that, isn't there a family here with some sort of 'love' or was it the 'love' of that extra money? It bothered me at first, but I accepted the fact that it was their trying to show me what life was like in the outside world and how tough it is. So much for life's lessons, I paid my dues already, I thought. I biked to a few restaurants in the area and ate there, it cost me less than the $20.00 I had been paying, but I guess I still 'loved' my gram. I had been so 'Grandmotherized', that the food the restaurants served did not taste at all like my gram's and it seemed hardly fit to eat. So, I returned to my 'relative's restaurant'. I paid my $20.00 per week and enjoyed it!

My love is like that

……..of a fire to a tree,
starting with a spark
burning slow at first
then engulfing all of you
yet never tasting your bark,
leaving you with a charred memory..
of me.

Changing At The Workfront

Back to work at the high school. Coach Johnny G., who played a large part in getting me hired, decided to change his profession from working with young men and their athletic abilities, to selling insurance. Another coach, Mr. Miller, a German bachelor, loner, with an attitude, in his early fifties became the new head coach. There was something this coach did not like about me and he made me aware of it from the start. I am not full of myself by any means, but personally, I think he was bitten by the envy bug. The reason for that was, when many of the students were in the office, they gravitated nearer to my desk and talked to me while he sat in his corner and read a book; it's possible. One of my duties was to take care of the previously mentioned Lob-ster tennis machine, when I was on my break. I would go out to the machine and play with some of the students. We all learned about tennis and even more important was the social skills that go along with this great game. There are some people who never learn how to do anything but try and live with themselves and they have plenty of trouble even doing that. This introverted head coach took it upon himself to find a way to get me fired from my job. They did not fire me but had my position taken away from the P.E. department and put me in the custodial department. I did not appreciate this move but what can a brain trauma victim do but go with the flow. Talk about boring; pushing brooms and emptying garbage cans was not what I thought I was meant to do in life. This same head custodian was there when I attended high school and his rotten reputation had not changed one bit. As a matter of fact, it had gotten worse. And most of the 'nasty' things said about him were affirmed by several of the students that I had taken care of while they were in my athletic training office in the gym. I knew he liked the young girls at school and some

84

of the comments spoken validated my thoughts. I wanted to confront him, but I knew it was in my best interest to keep my mouth shut. I did for a while, but then a few of the young ladies came up to me and asked me what they should do about this position they were put in. I told them to talk to their counselors because he was my boss and whatever I might say would put me in a bad position, job-wise. But off the record, I told them some possibilities they could do to improve their situation. I truly did not care; I did not like this job. Well, as life would have it, again, they moved me to another position within the district. The football field next to Pacific High School, which was our rival way back when, seven years ago, was a long time when you are only 25.

Within

Looking at that lovely girl
With her long and luscious grin
And every time I gaze at her
My heart begins to spin.
As she speaks with so much life
Within the air around
I cannot hear a single word
But yet the feeling is found.
Her eyes tell a story
And yes they light a fire
Within my soul, it tingles so
It is she whom I desire.

I Tried To Do It On My Own, Bad Choice!

This change, I thought, brought on another drastic event in my life. I began to think that my drug, Dilantin, was messing up my life so I stopped taking this downer, cold turkey. Not a prudent thing to do. About a week and a half later while at work, I felt ill and told Andy, my boss, I needed to go home. DMV had recently received reinstated of my driver's license. My mother had sold me her '69 Firebird. I drove it back to my apartment. I called my mother and tried to talk to her, but I did not make much sense, and she realized that something was wrong. She drove down from her Hayward office, picked me up and took me to Eden Hospital. En route, I had a seizure, a petite mal, where my left side went weird. I remembered from reading in a first aid manual that putting your head down between your legs, will not allow you to swallow your tongue. Mom had seen my grand mal seizures, but these petite mals were new to this 'experienced in life' mom. She told me to hang on and we would soon be there. I took it to be another step in life.

I was admitted to Eden Hospital; from there I was taken to an observation room where I had several more petite mal seizures. An R.N. named Nancy came in and questioned how I was feeling, just as I was having another episode. She was very attractive and looked like one of my seizures, petite.

In The Hospital Again

I awoke in another hospital room totally confused as to why I was here again. In the back of my scrambled brain, I knew, but I needed another explanation, and there was my dear mom. She told me what happened and what, from her point of view, was going on. I went through another battery of tests all pointing to the fact that I was under-medicated. I could have told them that, but I never did. I had to try and see if I could get off the medicine, my way. If I had asked, the doctors might have agreed with me, but no, I did it the hard way. This cost me another year without driving, I am not the brightest star in the sky!

Back on the bicycle again, my trusty yellow Schwinn and myself, off to work at the football field, mowing, raking, watering, and field lining day after day. I brought my own lunch every day because there was no lunchroom at the facility, only an upper-middle-aged man and myself. I was his sidekick/ helper, and a hot in the summer, cold in the winter, storage shed. We kept everything in this trailer. Phil was a quiet, never-get-excited, type of man. He knew what he was talking about and when he was on a break, he constantly listened to KGO, a talk radio program. We had a little Italian boss, Mike, about 5'4", who had worked at the Oakland Coliseum. He was very smart; I guess that is why he was the boss and Phil and I were the 'grunts'. About the only thing different from this job than my position as custodian at SLHS were the location and the bosses. I preferred working with the youth rather than lawn mowers and fertilizer. You have to earn a living when you are in these United States. So, I rode my bike back and forth from home to work every day for nearly a year. I must admit, the bicycle is a great way to improve your health physically and mentally. I rode anywhere from 7 to 25 miles a day. My blood pressure, at its lowest and best, was 105/60 and my pulse was 50. I was proud of that fact but I still walked liked I had one too many. It was just me!

Was A Nursing Job A Possibility?

I was reading our daily newspaper after work one evening and saw a want ad stating that if you would like to better yourself, become a nursing assistant. You can help your fellow human beings by taking care of them, using the skills taught at this small medical-help school. I thought to myself that this sounded interesting and maybe worth looking into. The following day, I hopped on my bike, took BART, our Bay Area Rapid Transit System, to Fremont. I rode to the school, near my favorite Uncle Bert's fabric store, got off my bike and went inside the building. I went in the lobby and was a little nervous about trying something new. I forged on! I saw a young lady dressed in white and I spoke first asking, "Is this the right building to inquire about the nurse assistant training school"? She said yes it was, so I asked if she was the right person to talk to about my enrolling. She said she would get the correct person, right away. Then, out came this middle-aged woman. She started asking me a large group of questions, who, what, where, when and why? I particularly liked the why question. It was then I repeated my age-old auto-accident story where I told her of my desire to help my fellow humans. I guessed she was either impressed or the school needed more students and money. Anyway, I was in another venture on this rocky road of life.

I started school the following week. I purchased a new wardrobe of white clothes. The thought of me in white! I will be washing these clothes until the cows come home. I was glad that my landlord paid for the cold water anyway. I took BART and my yellow Schwinn bike to my new school of semi-higher-learning. I was the first to enter the classroom and there I waited for my fellow classmates. I wondered who else would take on this new employment chapter in life. The first one enter was a middle-aged woman. Naturally, I introduced myself. She was Diane, and we started to speak about the class and what we expected to get from it. Then another lady, several years younger than I, was the next to enter, and smiled as she came into the room. Smiles always attract me! The three of us introduced ourselves (her name was Gwen) and continued talking about our new class. A rather small woman dressed in white came into the room. She introduced herself as Betty. The badge on her chest said she was an R.N.. I had my fill of RNs in my life; what's another one in the whole picture of things?

I went to nursing school, a far cry from the orthodontist I had one day dreamed of becoming. At least it was in the same area of life that I wanted to be, helping my fellow man. School was harder than I thought, learning how to interact with the patients, doctors and regulations. Some of the places on the human body I thought were 'sacred' were only, according to Betty, spots of normal bodily functions. I learned plenty from her. During the schooling, we practiced what we learned at an adult-care nursing facility almost next door to the school, how convenient that was. One of the first things I did was the TPR concept, temperature, pulse and respiration. We first took the pulse of about ten patients; some were more difficult than others. The older generation definitely has its difficulties! One of their problems is, they are many times slower to react. I had trouble taking the pulse on several of the 'larger' elderly gentlepeople. Some laughed and made a fun game of it, I liked working with that type of patient, while others gave me a terribly hard time. I don't know if it was the fact that they could see that I was a 'rookie' and they played on the fact or that they were simply being hard headed and did not want to cooperate. Thank goodness my smile and a small touch of humor helped me through those difficult times.

It was time for more information out of my textbooks. I studied until I thought my eyes would fall out. The older generation, as I found out, needed more care than I thought they did. I had no idea how much work was involved in their care. It turns out I was ill-informed about the aged, yet, I knew I was not a quitter, so I continued with my new schooling. I think I did most of this only to prove I could finish something without the help of anyone but me, a carryover from the pre-accident Dave. I did not want to become a social leech or worse yet, a parental sponge, living off my folks for the rest of my life. It did not work for me, others maybe, but me, I don't think so. I thought I was brought into this world to do something with myself. I wanted to make my parents proud of this young man, one who was still in the continuing process of finding out who he actually was and what his purpose was in life. I stayed with the program. I learned about the caring, what to do and what not to do. In many phases concerning their well-being, I was very competent and there were a few occasions when I was at a loss. My mind usually remembered the BIG important issues but the details, not so well. That is when my instructor came to my rescue. My mishap left me with a 'Swiss cheese' type memory. I could be told something one minute and then two or three minutes later, I'd forget. Fortunately, we had our books nearby so we could check out and find the correct response. Seeing it in print helped to solidify it inside my cranium. With myself and many other head-traumatized victims, repetition, repetition, repetition, was a necessary procedure to accommodate certain situations. It had to be done or the task was non-attainable. In my case, once a problem has been solved, for the most part, it will stay inside my head for the remainder of my existence.

Working in an 'old folks' home' was not what I thought I was cut out for, but it was a great learning experience. It is only another phase in the life I led. I did it without the problem of seeing blood and guts. I had seen much of that while I was hospitalized from my trauma.

A New Job Opportunity

I completed my schooling at Med-Help and passed the final. I was told that there was a hospital, the Masonic Home, which would hire me right away. It was a large convalescent facility on Mission Boulevard in Hayward. I went there within the following week and was I shocked at the response I got from the lady in charge of hiring. I got an appointment, went to her office as requested, knocked on her door, and entered. In my normal way of proceeding, with my uneven gait, got to the chair by her desk and sat down. The first thing out of her mouth was, instead of, "Good morning, how are you today?" was, "WHY DO YOU LIMP?" I was taken completely off guard by her lack of compassion and said, I had surgery. She continued, "What kind of surgery"? I normally do not get irritated at much of anything, "I had brain surgery." I hoped it would shut her up and prayed she would get on with her non-gratifying miserable job. She then said, "We cannot hire you because anything you might do may injure the patients and they would hold the hospital responsible." She then showed me to the door. I was surprised that she did not take her foot out of her mouth and kick me with it. She must like the taste of toes. I came home again, dejected!

From there, I tried working at a convalescent hospital near my apartment. I was there for a week and the head nurse called me into her office. I was told I was too slow, and I was, as they put it ever so gently, let go.

A Real Place Of Employment

I was completely perturbed with the whole world. They told me things that didn't always come true and when they did occur, it was not always like I hoped. I guess the old expression comes into place, "Life is what happens to you when you are making other plans!" I still wanted to work at a hospital, so I put my job application in at Eden Hospital, in Castro Valley, CA. I had been comatose in this institution for several months. I came home and 'forgot' about my job appointment. About two weeks later, I received a letter in the mail stating they wanted me to come speak to the person in charge of hiring. I was there before they took another breath. When I got to my possible new employer, they told me I would be working in the Burn Unit. I did not realize that you had to be extremely quick, mentally and bodily. I was okay mentally, but speed was not in my vocabulary. I lost that the day of my wreck, but I was not going to tell them, they would have to find that out for themselves. I don't like the expression, to lie, and I never do, I guess I did not reveal the whole truth. I started on the AM shift, 7-3pm which was the best for me, I liked the morning shift as my concentration is better in then. It dwindles towards the afternoon, a reminder of my hospital days.

The Working World

There was a group of six new employees, all ready to take on their new jobs, from nurse assistants to R.N.'s. We were told that the first several days would have us learning the scope of the hospital, from the burn unit on the sixth floor, to the morgue in the basement. I took notes to help me get everything straight in my mind, a difficult task for any new employee. Out of all the floors, I liked the floor with the teenagers on it. I seem to gravitate towards the 'middle-aged 'youth. This is probably the reason that those were the years that were eliminated from my mind. I guess I wanted to re-live them through these youngsters. When the week was finally over, I had so much information thrown at me I could hardly remember my name. But I could tell you which floor pediatrics was on. When we got to the Burn Unit, we had to put on gowns over our street clothes so that we would not contaminate the patients with germs from the outside world. So this was going to be my new home for 'hopefully' the rest of my days. Hospitals are what most everyone dreads. I was as observant as I could be, taking as many notes about this section of the hospital. We saw several patients, all with many different type burns. They ranged from an explosion victim, burned around his face and upper torso to a black man who was 98 years old, fell asleep in bed, smoking. He woke up in the hospital with 95% of his body charred and terribly burnt. All I could see were his eyes, part of his nostrils, and the right side of his mouth, the rest of his body was covered in bandages. The following Monday, I was to start my 'real' full-time job.

I got to work about fifteen minutes before I was supposed to just to make sure I was at the right place. Hoping this was honestly a real job or if this was a fantasy, hopefully the former! I went to the sixth floor burn unit, got in my blue cotton 'jumpsuit', entered the nurses' office and reported in. The head R.N. was sitting at her desk, I guessed or hoped she was waiting for my arrival. She looked up from her writings, smiled and said, "Can I help you?" I introduced myself and said, "I guess I am your newest employee, where do I belong?" She requested one orderly, Ray, to come show me the ropes and many procedures I needed to follow to perform up to my job's qualifications. He showed me every corner of each room of the sixth floor burn unit in the hospital. It stretched what was left of my brain, to the maximum. I was hired for a trial period of ninety days and then I was supposed to get a review to see if I was able to get hired on permanently. I started work, cleaning the tubs where the R.N.'s removed the burnt dead skin from the bodies of the patients in order for new skin to grow. I also talked to the patients about their lives and what and how their mishaps occurred, not prying but in a gentle way to satisfy my own curiosity. I did the PM and the Graveyard shifts. One night there was a full moon, it was the end of the month, and there were eight corpses to come into the ER department. I wrapped and brought them down to the 'cooler'. When you have a dead body, you wrap it in a sheet with its face showing so that it looked like there was only an unconscious body being pushed around. No one asked me any questions and I told them no fibs, concerning their state of mind or lack of it. I don't mean to make light of a grave situation, but I consider them rather fortunate not to have the struggles we mortals must endure. We must wait until our creator, whomever we believe Him or her to be, calls us home.

This was a challenge to say the least. Never in my young life had I seen the trials and turmoil that the body human goes through to stay as well as it does. I saw pain, heard screams when the bodies were going under the knife for dead skin removal, debriding. I also saw peace and relief when the procedure was completed.

I was there for a total of eighty-eight days until the head nurse called me into her office and gave me the 'word'. I knew it would come someday and I had almost made it to the end of my probation period, possibly. I had done my work well enough that I might get hired permanently. She stated that I was too slow for the job and they, instead of firing me would give me another chance by retraining me within a two-day time period. Now the question is, how do you learn a new job that took eighty-eight days to get down, then they show you how to do it all over again in two days? A little bit impossible, what did they think I was, normal or something? I told them when they first hired me that I was slow, what did they expect, miracles? I performed one miracle, waking up and I am no magician. As I thought, they told me it was over, pack my bags and it was time to head out. So, I said good-bye to a few of the patients who I had befriended and went on to another life phase, in this same slow body.

I came back to my apartment, shed a tear or two and continued on with my life. I went to several hospitals in the area, filled out job applications and waited for their replies. I did not even get a postcard saying "Thanks for your interest. We cannot use your services right now, come back again when we have an open position." I learned the many things a Nurse Assistant needs to know in order to accomplish each task, the only thing wrong with that is my speed. I have two speeds, slow and stop. If I put it in reverse, I usually fall down.

Another Chance

I went to the Hick'ry Pit for breakfast; I was lazy and didn't like to cook. So, I ordered one scrambled egg, an English muffin and water, call me cheap. But, when I was with my dad on Sundays after church, I got a big meal of two scrambled eggs, sausages and toast. Dad and I talked about the past week and plans for the one upcoming. While there, I met several pleasant people. My dad, who was a storeowner from down the street, knew most of them already. One was a waitress, Jean, who had a son. She told us about him and his accident. He broke his neck in a trucking accident and was paralyzed from the neck down. Dad went home, and I went to meet Jean's son in his apartment down the street from the restaurant. Upon coming to his place, I knocked, then, entered when he said come in. I was a little surprised at his condition but I knew for the most part what I was to expect. He was there with a young lady named Deb and their son. I believed she was his ex-wife. We introduced ourselves. He was Jer. We started talking about my possible new job, working with a quadriplegic. I knew the job but I did not know the person with whom I was to start taking care. Jer went to my rival high school and we graduated the same year. He looked okay from the head up but from the neck down, his body looked limp and lifeless, 'normal' for his condition. We exchanged thoughts and desires and then we agreed on my new position; I finally had a job as an attendant for a quad. This was not the orthodontist like I had planned, but I was at least working with my fellow 'Earth Mates'. I was to start on the following Monday.

That Monday, I hopped on my bicycle and rode into my fair city of San Leandro, about four and a half miles down the road. I went to his apartment, knocked and went in. I greeted him, emptied the urine bag, bathed, dressed, and set him up in his wheelchair for the day to come. Jer had an electric wheelchair and a unique way about him. He taught me things about the way a quad gets things done that my teachers at my Nurse Assistant School never got across. The school taught us many of the large concepts of how to take care of totally disabled people. There are many individualities that a NA can learn, only by practically living with these disabled people. I have come to the conclusion that when GOD made us, he did it in the way that we are all special with certain gifts that accompany this entire bodily package.

Every day, I would pedal into town; stop at my favorite 'watering hole', the Hick'ry Pit for my usual scrambled egg, water and English muffin. This was served by a cute little waitress named Debbie, who was the daughter of the hostess,

Annette. Annette went to high school with my dad, this was a small world. My meal cost $1.35. I would leave a fifty-cent tip. Boy, was I a big spender! I finished my meal, boarded my bicycle and continued the trip to Jer's apartment. I got off, locked my bike to a fence, knocked on the door, identified myself, and then walked into the front room. Jer was in the back, in his bed with urine bag connected to the side rail of his bed. I emptied it into the toilet, cleaned it out, flushed, and reattached it to the bed. I got warm water for his bed bath, along with his towel, washcloth, and soap. Every morning I would give him his bed bath from head to toe this included every crevice along the way. That was what I was trained to do and I did it to the best of my abilities. We talked about our lives before our mishaps, the struggles we had to try and overcome, the memories we lost, the new information we had to process.

Almost Back To My San Leandro Ways

Jer would often offer to buy me lunch. He had changed his way of eating, from a carnivore to almost a vegetarian, saying it seemed to digest better within his fragile system. It happened that a wonderful vegetarian shop opened about two blocks from Jer's apartment. I told him about it as I saw it change from a men's store to a fine eating establishment. It was called Cessy's Pantry and it opened up on East 14th, near Jer's apartment. They sold everything: the organic style with the freshest fruit to the finest sandwiches a person like Jer would eat for lunch. I brought it back to his place and we feasted on these delicious delicacies. I asked if all was done to his liking. He agreed and then I walked out the door to my bicycle. I unlocked it, put on my hat, hopped on my mode, and pedaled on down the road, homeward bound. En route, I had my needs, such as saying hello to all my friends who were always there. Some, face to face and some who prayed for me while I was unconscious a few years back. I stopped at Fabric Lane, my dad and uncle's business, the folks there always greeted me with open arms. Next door was Loudy's Jewelry. Fran, and his wife, Marge, have been my friends for many, many years. Warren, the Mobile gas station car washer, where dad got fuel for his station wagon every week and always had a joke to share. He was a lovely man who wouldn't hurt a flea. He could clean your car like nobody I have ever seen. He never made fun of me like some people did, he just accepted me as I was. That one of the reasons I appreciated him as much as I did. I stopped to see Doug at Blaisdells' Stationery Shop next door to my Fabric Lane, who was another wonderful human being who gave me support when I was down for the count. Then, there was San Leandro Savings, with the cutest tellers in the county. After, it was back to the ol' homestead, my apartment on 163rd Avenue.

Didn't Miss The Bus, The Bus Gave Me The Squeeze!

One morning on the way to my patient's apartment, near 150th Avenue, I was pedaling my normal speed when an Alameda County Transit Bus passed me. I noticed it had its turn signal on and it was about to stop at the bus stop about thirty feet ahead of me. The bus began to come towards my bicycle lane. It cut me off and stopped right in front of me. As it did, I squeezed my hand brakes as tight as I could. It was too little, too late. It cornered me between the bus and the curb, causing me to fly off my bike. The most fortunate thing about this incident was, I am pretty good with numbers and memory of them. Just as the bus was sending me sailing, while in flight, I looked up and saw the rear end of the vehicle and the numbers upon the back, and made a mental note of it. Several people saw what happened and offered me assistance. I thanked them, said I was OK, as far as I knew. Then, I looked at my only mode of getting around and saw my front rim was bent beyond recognition, my handlebars were twisted and for the most part, my riding confidence had 'sprung a leak'. I called my grandmother, since she was my apartment manager, and told her what happened. She offered to come and bring me home. We brought the mutilated frame of my bike back to my apartment, evidence of the mishap.

As soon as I got back to my home, I opened the phone book and looked up the AC Transit number, then dialed it. I asked for the correct department concerning my mishap. I related my story about what had occurred. They were very gracious and told me to send the bill for my bicycle and doctor visit if I needed it. I don't think they wanted a lawsuit. I never would have sued, but they didn't know that. I took my heap of a bike to Amaral Cyclery in town, the same place I bought the bicycle several years before. It cost $140. They repaired my vehicle for less than $100 and it worked like new; they even repainted parts where it was needed. They did an excellent job and I applauded them for diligence and speed.

I got the receipt, paid the bill then sent the receipt to AC Transit. About a week later they sent me a check covering the entire transaction, no questions asked. They were better than I expected.

After The Bicycle Mishap

A few months later I was visiting my old hospital, going from ward to ward like I did for several years after my leaving there. I saw Mr. Amaral laying in one of those dreaded hospital beds. He was a patient in H building. He had a severe stroke which I did not think he would recover. He smiled as he recognized me, we talked a little, and I shook his palsied hand and said goodbye. I knew this would be the last time I would see him.

My Bus Encounter

I called my mom and tried to explain what had happened and she freaked, asking, was I OK? Did I need anything? I told her I needed a large plastic shell to protect me from this ugly world that seemed out to get me. The next day, she dropped by with a brand new orange/red BELL motorcycle helmet. It took a while to get used to this heavy, light bulb shaped contraption used for my protection. It worked perfectly for many years. People could see me coming for miles. I am not usually an extrovert, but I liked being noticed. I do not like to have people think that there goes a guy who has struggled to make something of himself, without asking for much. All they need to do is only accept me as another fellow human being.

I called Jer's home and said I was in an accident, told him what had happened. He said take it easy for the rest of the day. He then told me he would ask Deb to come over and take care of him. I said thanks and I will take the bus to work tomorrow while my bike is in *its* hospital. The next day, I took the bus to Jer's. Actually, I prefer the wind blowing in my face rather than having another bus riding, heavy breathing passenger blow their stale breath up my nose. So much for my preferences. I took the bus for a week. My bike was probably the only thing to help keep my sanity. It was a stress release for me. When I rode on it, I had to concentrate mainly on my balance but it was a 'necessity' to see who I was riding past. I had to look at almost everyone I encountered. In my travels one day, a pretty young thing in a mini skirt with shapely long legs caught my eye while I was approaching an intersection. I did not notice the light changing before I was into the crosswalk. I glanced up right in the nick of time to see a fast moving auto almost on top of me. He missed me by that (   ) much; so much for my watching the girls.

I Thought I Was Smelling A Rat

Over a year passed while I was working for Jer. During this time, I noticed his personality was changing. When I first met him, he was accepting and easy to get along with, but as the weeks turned to months, something was changing about him. I was doing my duties with my patient when there was a ring at the front door. This was unusual, Jer never had callers before noon except for Deb, and she was 'family'. This person brought a bag of what looked like oregano, the spice, what did I know? I had seen but I had never smoked the substance, I had my suspicions, but I have smelled it. When it was lit, it was nasty and it turned my stomach. I recalled that pungent fragrance. I thought, should I question Jer about this or let it slide under the rug? My conscious told me to ask him flat out, after all honesty is the best policy. So I asked him, "Do you do drugs? Is this marijuana yours"?

He said, "Yes."

"How often do you do drugs?"

He said, "Daily."

I mentioned that I noticed his changing personality over the past few months and it bothered me. I thought he was his own person and he knew better after all that he had been through. I also told him with the mess your body has been in, the paralysis, I imagined you had it under control.

WRONG GUESS! His demeanor changed, taking a radical switch. He stated very indignantly, "What business is it of yours anyway?"

I told him I was his caregiver and I was doing my best to keep him as healthy as I could for his condition. He attempted to convince me that it was good for him. I tried to tell him that it was not at all good for him and that he should stop this foolishness. I would not be able to take care of him anymore.

He said, "That is too bad, I need this to control my pain."

I replied, "It is the dope or me."

He responded, "The marijuana makes me feel better than you ever could."

I told him that his marijuana won't clean his urine bag or bathe him, either. I gathered up my equipment, and walked out the front door. I did not look back. I got on my bike and instead of taking the usual route and talking to the same crowd, I went up to Fairmont Hospital.

Good Advice From My Friend

I went to my 'wake up ward', C2, and began a conversation with Ms. Mick, head R.N. for the day shift in the intensive care unit. She was a wonderfully strong but sensitive woman who seemed to have a sixth sense about patients. I found it impossible to put one over on her. As I look back, I have come to realize that she was in charge of dozens of other nurses, orderlies and maintenance people. This gave her plenty of eyes to see the whole picture from many angles, of different personalities. It helped her to make many decisions from the observations she was given. I couldn't get away with anything. She was always well-informed. She knew something was troubling me. Ms. Mick reassured me that I had made the correct decision to leave the whole situation behind.

When I came home for Christmas, the first time after my mishap, she was almost at my bedside before I got there. She was one of the most well-informed persons with nursing skills to see me the entire day. I had dozens of well-wishers drop by to see if it was truly the same old David who was always there with a smile on my face. All 120 pounds of me sat in my wheelchair, patch over my eye and a different look about me. The only one who knew it was me for sure was our dog, Kelly. She did what she did when her supper was ready. She sat up on her haunches in a pretty way, the minute she saw me coming up the stairs. I could almost see a little tear in her eye, everybody was glad to see me, almost as glad as I was to be home. I was not at all embarrassed by my condition. I was a strapping young man weighing in at a grand total of 120 pounds, 6'1" tall, wheelchair-bound, with a 'Rooster Cogburn' patch covering my bad eye. This was the first time I was allowed to come back to the home front. Taking this fragile, skinny young man and having him end up on another bed, a convertible sofa type, in our den. Dad brought home my wheelchair in his '68 Chevy station wagon. He set it up in the den near our Serta perfect sofa bed so when I got tired, which was an easy thing for me to do even after a four-month nap.

More Memories Of Yesterday

When I started waking up, I began to yawn. From what my friends said, these yawns were BIG YAWNS. They seem to last for minutes at a time. After a while, these people used to carry on about them, Moe and Ellie in particular. They said they had never seen such a big, gaping hole the size of mine in their entire lives. I could not help it, they just came out naturally. I would yawn dozens of times in only an hour. I must have held the Guinness world record for the yawning event. My yawning was my 'trademark' for many months. What a way to be remembered!

Back To The Real World

I went to my 'old home away from home', Fairmount Hospital C-2 ward and started talking to my old friends, patients as well as nurses. I noticed a new patient sitting in wheelchair so I went up to him and told him my story and he told me his. In our conversation, he informed me that he was soon to be out of the hospital and ready to go home. He would need an attendant. I told him I had recently gotten my certificate from the state. I was certified to be a nursing assistant. I gave him my phone number and told him if he might be interested in my help to give me a call as soon as he got his walking papers, oops! rolling papers. He got the permission of the hospital and moved out about four miles from my apartment going eastward. It was the opposite direction from Jer's place, nearly the same distance. Lee moved into a small house in Hayward. He had a ramp built up to the front door and so started my new endeavor. Lee was a larger man than Jer, so it took a lift to move him from the bed to his chair. This was one of the many things

I learned how to do in my 'mini medical school'. He had an older van with a lift for his wheelchair.

While at Fairmont Hospital, he had met a young lady, Joy, of African American decent, who had a son, Lamar. The three bonded and they moved into the house together. Joy was a sturdy, small lady who seemed to keep continually busy and became more so even after I started working there. Lamar was eight years old, small like his mom, smart, but like most boys his age, a little scattered. Lee was strict when it came to discipline and schooling. He knew all the tricks from his previous marriage. He made sure Lamar got his homework done and up to par every day. He was a good father figure for a man in his condition. He had to do this for the shortcomings Lamar suffered without a father figure through in his younger life.

Doing It On The 'Lee'-Ward Side

On the way to work every morning, I'd stop at the old Foster Freeze restaurant where in the late Fifties my family had gone for an occasional ten-cent frosty treat. How good can you get! It had now turned into Maria's Kitchen, where they served marvelous Mexican meals at this terrific 'down casa' café. I would order an egg on a tortilla instead of an English muffin and water. Sometimes I might add an extra tortilla with a pat of butter and jelly if I was hungrier than usual. This was an odd combination, but consider the source: the guy with the strange taste buds. After finishing my meal I'd pay my bill, go out the door, put on my helmet, hop on my bike and finish my ride to Lee's house. When I got to Lee's house, I'd take my bike up on his disabled ramp, park it near his front door, go up to it give my usual friendly knock and enter. Again, I would go through my normal routine.

I'd clean, drain and dress the patient, put him in his chair, readying him for the upcoming day he was about to face. Lee was probably one of the most intelligent patients I have taken care of in my entire nursing career. He told me that he was a short-haul trucker and a union man. He also made me think that if I did anything that displeased him in any way, whether orally or bodily, he would have me taken care of by one of his 'brothers'. That scared me for about 30 seconds but my good ol' short -term memory kicked in and I forgot about the whole thing. But, I made sure I never would find out the validity concerning his so-called threats. During one week of my care, while Joy was out of town for something that had to do with her employment, Lee asked me if I would stay about 24 hours a day at his place and take care of him for the while Joy was gone. She would be gone for two weeks. I obliged and took the offer. I trusted his word of giving me double what I normally was getting for my usual time. That sounded good, almost too good but I decided to take it anyway. Lee let me take off in the middle of the day to do some of the personal things I had to do while Joy's son, Lamar, watched him. I returned to his place so I could prepare dinner. I felt more like a butler, maid and servant than an attendant. I also felt compelled to complete this job knowing that I would be compensated. My duties included waking every two hours so I could turn Lee from one position to another. If I would have known that it was going to be this exhausting, I would have never started it. I slept on his sofa with an alarm clock by my side. Every two hours it would startle me up and out of a deep sleep, which I always seemed to go into whenever I laid my head upon my pillow. I would get up, go to his room, turn him, and give him a sip of water or whatever he needed. I went back to my couch, set the alarm clock then returned to my 'near coma' state for two more hours until my next rude awakening. I recall one night I was tired beyond belief. I knew it was my 'duty' to be at his call every time the alarm went off. I forgot to set the clock for the usual two hours, and I got two hours and 45 minutes of the most needed repose. Lamar came in and started shaking my shoulder and softly saying David, wake up, then, that small lad scolded me for not doing my job. When I got my bearings, I arose and went to Lee's room he almost raised the roof concerning my ineptness as to my duties. I apologized up and down explaining I had forgotten to set my alarm clock. I then was instructed to check his body over for new bed sores that might have happened within the extra 45 minutes I let pass without turning his precious body. I don't especially like to be made a fool when I try my hardest to keep a person pleased and content. I am doing it for almost nothing! What can one expect? I was in a quandary as what to do, so, I stuck it out until the end of the two week's pay period. Lee brought the money to the dinner table where we always went at pay time. He told me to get the money out of his pocket, where Joy put it. He handed me the envelope and waited for my reaction. I was expecting to get the amount we decided on before we began this endeavor. It was $20.00. I then asked him if this was a joke because I did not think it was the least bit funny. He told me in his sternest voice that this was all he thought I was worth for the past weeks. I tried to tell him I was at his beck and call for almost 24 hours a day for an entire two weeks and all I earned was $20.00. I don't think so. I got out of my chair, went out the front door, got on my bike and went home. I tried to guess what I did wrong to make him turn on me like that. So much for we, disabled folk trying to help to improve their lives by giving so much of ours.

'Post' Lee

After the incident with Lee, I decided to go back to Chabot, to get into a poetry class, in my opinion, one of the favorite things I do. I enrolled in class and waited for that day to arrive. The evening came and class began. It appeared that it was going to be just another poetry class, no sparks, only verse. Wouldn't you know it, the second January evening, there was a huge storm along with a power failure; class was cancelled. I did not know what was waiting for me out there, but something was. The next Wednesday, class was to finally start. I got into my '72 Mercury Montego, went to school and walked up to my classroom. I was one of the first to arrive, so I sat down in the rear of the class and waited for Mr. Albert to get to his podium. While there, I observed a variety of people enter; young adults to people in their 70's. It happened that one of the young ladies who came was a sister of one of my middle sister's friends, and I had played tennis with her two summers before. Her name was Suzanne. She saw me, came over and sat beside me. We hugged and I asked, "What have you been doing with yourself?" She immediately corrected me, her name was not Suzanne, but Zanne. I said I was sorry for the mistake. She told me not let it happen again. I thought to myself, time brings changes and it did. I came home feeling like I might have an 'old new' friend to talk to.

And Then Out Of The Blue, An Angel

I returned to school the next week and I was sitting in the room early again, when, out of the blue, a young lady came into the room and she sat down right next to me. Now, what do I do? I looked over her way just to see why in the world anyone would want to sit next to me? I was the only one in the class. I had a bit of an inferiority problem within me. She smiled at me and I thought, *hmmm kinda cute...*but what would she want with me? She introduced herself as Mary Jo. I responded that I was David. I asked where was she from. She said New York. I questioned, "You actually came all the way from New York to take a California poetry class?" She smiled and responded, "No, I took this class to get away from my 8:00-4:00 work environment." I again questioned, "Where do you work?" She said, Friden. I replied, "My grandmother Kay, worked at Friden when it was in San Leandro." She responded that she worked in the billing office in Hayward.

Then came the trick question: she asked, "Have you ever been to La Imperial Mexican Restaurant in Hayward?" I said no. She said, "And you have lived here all your life and you haven't gone to La Imperial?" She then asked if I would like to go. I thought, 'wow', a young lady would actually like to have dinner with me, what's wrong here? Is this all a dream? I mentally pinched myself and orally agreed to go out with her. I asked her where she lived so I could pick her up. She gave me her address I wrote it down along with her phone number just in case I got lost, me lost? Heaven forbid!

At class break, we went to the student center and had a little pick me up to get us through until class was over. I did not need anything because I was flying higher than an eagle. I was tickled beyond description; I was actually going out on a date with a pretty little thing.

Am I Going To Tell My Mother...About You!

I waited until I got home to call my mother and tell her the great news. It was late, so I called her in the morning. "Mom, guess what happened last night? I met a girl in my poetry class and she is great. We talked for what seemed like hours but it was only minutes. She is from a small town in New York, called Waverly. She has a big family with five brothers and sisters and two parents who have been married for forty-plus years, a long, long time. Isn't that remarkable in these days? What struck me most about her was that she did not even notice my limp. That is one thing most young women would want to know about, right up front and she is not oblivious. I like her already!" Again the good ol' mother support system came into play when she said, "That's wonderful, don't rush things, if you like her enough and she likes you things will work out, watch and see." I hung up smiling about the past evening and my stroke of such good luck.

Mary Jo gave me her work phone number and told me to call her around lunch if I wouldn't mind. I, being terribly excited at the chance of talking to this new acquaintance, called her the next day at the requested time. We talked for almost her entire lunch time about what was going on in her life, friends, family and what was she doing this evening. She invited me for dinner at her place. What a difference to my Kraft macaroni and cheese and Star Kist tuna! She fixed her own spaghetti quick sauce and pasta with Italian bread. The sauce was a little hot and too much salt for my taste buds. I thank the maker of Parmesan cheese, a lifesaver, or rather a tongue saver.

While I was there, Mary Jo kept the conversation going the entire night. I noticed that during our talk at our class break at Chabot, but I guessed that was only a little nervousness coming out. Wrong. She was a 'talk-a-holic'. She could talk most people under the table, but that was fine with me. I do not talk that well but give me a piece of paper, pen, an idea then look out, poem time. It was getting late, she had to get to work the next morning. I gave her gentle kiss on the lips, thanked her for the delicious but 'warm cuisine', kissed her again, a little warmer this time, turned to the door and left. I walked through the dark hallway between the apartment complex, out the gate and into the parking lot. I got into my car, looked in the mirror and saw I was not dreaming. I tried to wipe the huge smile from my face, couldn't, started my Montego and drove home happier than I had been in years. I came down Mission Boulevard, and I almost passed my 163rd Avenue, I made a wide turn, right into my apartment complex. There was my grandma looking out her window right at me motioning me to come see her. Obediently, I followed her hand instruction and came to see her. I got the third degree plus two: who, what, why, when and where? I tried to make it sound like it was only a friend meeting another. I did not want to say I found the woman of my life. I liked her plenty but I could not let on too soon. I only told her enough to pacify her until she asked me again. I played it down, then I told her I was getting tired and needed my beauty sleep, she agreed and let me go. I did not fly into my apartment, I floated. I undressed, showered, brushed my teeth and off to dreamland I went. I don't usually dream but this night was different, I thought about her the entire night. I could not seem to get her off my mind, was this love or what? I could not say truly because I had never felt these emotions before—only in high school, and that was called 'teenage puppy love'. Even now I still have a fond remembrance of those days. I called her every time I thought I wanted to hear her calming voice. I guess she stole my heart and I wanted her to keep it, forever.

Crossroad To Your Heart

I have stumbled down many a path
But I am on the right one at present
Before that moment when we embraced
I prayed she wouldn't resent it.
That girl who hadn't quite kissed me
This feeling has come and passed
I wish that I might still be there
But no, it could not last.
For now our paths have finally crossed
I hope it will stay that way
From now until forever
Beginning with today.

At Least I Knew I Was In Love

About two weeks after we started going out I told her I loved her and I meant it, sincerely. I hoped and prayed that she would tell me she loved me too but, she said she 'liked' me a lot. I hated the word, like, it sounded so "and I care about you too, but let's wait a while before we get serious." So, I waited and waited and waited or so it seemed, forever. It was more than I could take. We ate out more times than staying home, she worked and I was on disability making a 'ton of money' (ha ha) so it all was good enough for a couple of 'semi-average citizens'. We frequented many eateries, some great, others okay, and most barely edible. Then one night between bites of a big burrito, it came out of her mouth, the three most sought after words I needed to hear for weeks and months, 'I love you'. I almost choked on my burrito. I asked, "Did I hear what I thought I thought I did?" She seemed to blush, but a blush is hard to see on olive skin and she replied, "Yes." I reached across the table, softly kissed her on the cheek. Deep inside my brain was saying, "Now take it slow, dummy!" Taking it slow meant, well I know what slow is, I had been slow for about ten years prior. Who could tell how many 'slow years' I would have left? Only my creator knows and he's not talking too loud about that subject.

I could not believe it: a young lady who I presumed actually cared enough for me to say she loved me. I was not going to let this one go. We went out to dinner about three to four times a week for nearly three months. We ate at the Blue Dolphin; I knew a member of the band, Daybreak, who played there, Jim. He was a boyfriend one of my classmates, Lisa, when I moved to San Leandro in eighth grade.

Then she got a terrific idea. We would eat at her place during the week, fixed by her own hands, and eat out on weekends. That would definitely help my pocketbook. She prepared spaghetti with a tasty tomato quick sauce. It was better than I could even think of making. I was impressed, but then again, I was young and inexperienced, it still was good. Besides an 'eat-a-thon' way of being together, we dated too. We danced at several clubs in our vicinity, and went to the mall and shopped. We went to Knowland Park in Oakland and we traveled to San Francisco to the zoo. We went to many of the things our diversified greater San Francisco Bay Area had to offer. I could tell I was growing fonder of her every day. I thought this is the one I want to spend the rest of my life with. I shivered with the idea because I knew what my mom and dad went through, my mom and stepdad, my mom's parents. I hate divorce and I was afraid that this would *naturally* happen to me. I didn't want to even conjure up this idea again. Into the back of my head it went.

Things Were Getting Warmer

We continued with the dating scene, going to Lake Tahoe in a rented cabin for a week with her sister and brother-in-law and their three-year-old daughter, Marisa. All the way from Waverly, New York, came Mary Jo's mom and dad, Mary and Joe. We gambled a little, swam, saw Englebert Humperdink and a few sights, went out for many meals, and did the tourist thing. Every day we were together brought us closer and closer. Love was fun.

My Real Dad Even Liked Her, And He Had Good Taste

We went to see my natural father, Dan and his wife Jan, in Arcata, California. He was a Lieutenant in the police force there, with many responsibilities. It seemed like he had more as a Lieutenant than as a beat cop in Fremont. We spent two days there. He was such uplifting man, I enjoyed their company immensely. He was intelligent and forceful and Jan was a great cook. They were always down to earth and a joy to be around. The best thing about them was they never belittled me at any time I was with them. They made me feel like I was part of the family, which in their eyes, I was. I still was a bit uneasy at first, whenever there was a big gathering. There were folks who knew me whom I never remembered meeting but they knew who I was. It could have been that I resembled Dan in several ways. I had some of his mannerisms, whenever he would get tickled about an event or happening, he would burst out in genuine laughter. I didn't see that very often in many families. He was an altogether much different man than the dear man who raised me. I love and respect them both. We had the same body shape and we were definitely related. Dan's parents, Rocky and Helen, had seen me in the beginning of my life, as a baby, but Mom and Dan were married too young and divorced soon after my arrival. I could see my resemblance in many of my new relatives. In some way, life begins to make sense when you finally get all the details about the who's, what's, where's, why's, and how's that you were never around to deal with from the beginning.

I enjoyed this new-found family I had now encountered. The two life styles were altogether miles apart in what they wanted out of this earthly world. I grew up with one and it became the one I wanted to be like, then I met the other and found out that it was as good as the other only much different. I know I am a combination of both. I guess that makes me a…HAPPY MEDIUM!

People Were Starting To Question Me...

We returned to our separate apartments and I knew something was in the air. Everyone accepted Mary Jo as easily as I did and then I started getting the biz, when's the BIG DAY? My first response was, never! Why ruin a good thing with marriage? I still had many thoughts left in my head concerning my dad and mom and the huge change they put their three children through. Maybe that's selfish of me, but when people make a commitment to one another, they should <u>never</u> let anything divert their attention from the goal of a lasting love. You must learn to accept change as much as you do your mate. It does not matter what situation may arise.

Echoes softly

Gently as my open mind
Travels through your field
Never could I find
That you may ever yield.
In your deepest garden
Or far down past your pond
Is where I'll meet this tender love
Right there and not beyond.
Calmly as we do embrace
This feeling that we share
Echoes softly in my mind
There is nothing to compare.

When You Have A Problem, Ask A Friend Or Two

I went to Fabric Lane one afternoon and talked to two dear friends I had known for over two dozen years. Ida was the cashier and Nita had been a secretary, for almost as long as the store was in operation. I could tell them anything I had on my mind and they wouldn't even flinch. They were more rocks I could stand on. In my own stuttering way, I told them individually, I thought I had fallen in love. I had never done this before, telling a person you care a lot about that you had fallen in love and wanted to marry. They were a touch surprised I would have such a wonderful thing to tell them. They were a few of the first to know this.

Before my letting anyone in my family know, I was not sure what my heart was telling me to do. Confusion was my middle name. They told me to take it slow and not to rush into anything too fast otherwise you could blow everything. Then you'd be back on lonely street and that was a dead end way to go. I said I think I could handle that but it would be so hard to do because she was better than I thought I might ever find. She wanted to have a life we could share. She is kind, giving, pretty and she didn't even notice I limped, that was a major selling point! I loved her terribly, more like wonderfully, but I had those recurring thoughts of my parents and their divorce pop into my head. I wanted those ideas to stop.

In the back of my mind, I wondered how I could create a unique way of asking this special lady if she would do me the honor of taking my hand. I wondered if I could write a poem, I knew I could write a piece of verse that might capture the moment, take her by surprise and win over her heart. So I got to thinking, I saw a poem where you read the entire verse then at the end you read the first letter of each line and a question appears.

I wrote................<u>W</u>.........
<u>I</u> ....
<u>L</u> ....
<u>L</u> ......
<u>Y</u> .....
<u>O</u> .....
<u>U</u>.....
<u>M</u>.....
<u>A</u>.....
<u>R</u>.....
<u>R</u>.....
<u>Y</u>.....
<u>M</u>.....
<u>E</u>.....
?

Now, I had to fill in the dots, so, I put on my thinking cap and came up with this......

> <u>W</u>hen you came into my life
> <u>I</u> did not know what to do
> <u>L</u>ittle did I know what lay ahead
> <u>L</u>ove was coming into view.
> <u>Y</u>esterday I was alone
> <u>O</u>f you my thoughts were deep
> <u>U</u>naccustomed as I was
> <u>M</u>y night would bring no sleep.
> <u>A</u>t dawn it finally came to me
> <u>R</u>enounce the single life you live
> <u>R</u>ejoice and share my love
> <u>Y</u>es is the only reply to give.
> <u>M</u>ary Jo, I love you so
> <u>E</u>ternally my love will grow.
> ?

I wrote it in calligraphy, a skill I had learned at an adult school in Castro Valley. I could not drive then, so Bonnie, the young lady who told me about the class came, picked me up and we went to school. Unfortunately, she was having marital troubles and she had to quit taking me after only two classes. I bought the books for the class and the pens needed to learn the beautiful writing skill. Prior to her stopping class, she gave me the board you use to perform your talent. The calligraphy board was a type of large clip board. It measured approximately 30" by 24". I guess I considered myself as the Abe Lincoln of calligraphy. I read the book on how to do the writings, practiced the art in my apartment for hours on end and now have the one style down to near perfection, my own.

I Knew How, But When Was My Dilemmna

Now I had to pick the right time to give this to her. My birthday was within the next few days so, I said to myself, wouldn't it be a perfect birthday gift to get her to say, yes, she will marry me on <u>my</u> day? A little selfish, but she'll never know. I knew it would be a lifetime gift and one that could not be exchanged. I showed my poem to my mother at her real estate office, and also to several of my friends along with the hopes of getting their approval of my choice of my life partner. They all agreed with me in thinking that she was the best I could ever want or need in my situation.

TIME IS AT HAND (and it was a-shakin'!)

Mary Jo asked me to come to her apartment for my birthday dinner. I knew in my heart I had to do this a bit on the sly side, so, I put the poem in a gold wooden frame. Then, I put it into a plastic bag and another so she would not know what I had up my sleeve. I arrived at her place, nervous as a cat on a warm skillet, and dreading a negative response. Most of the time, I am positive but in certain cases when your entire life is about to come to a screeching turn in the road; the cause being the…m.m.m.ar.ri..a..ge word. I stutter a little when I become nervous and when the pressure becomes even too much for me to handle, I get mad. Like I said before, if you make me angry, I can keep up with the best of them. I picked up the proposal off the car seat and got out of my Mercury Montego. I started to slowly walk into the back entrance of her apartment house. I was not shaking and my knees weren't wobbling, but it was as if I was walking on top of a group of eggs ready to hatch. When the chicks' heads pop out of their secure place, they would scare me enough to run back to my car. Then, I would return to my own safe place, my apartment. But then I asked myself, what kind of person are you who has to go hide behind Granny's skirt? Are you as tough as you once thought you were? Well, of course I am. I hope. So I went through the gate, I got to the door, said my little prayer, "Lord, give me strength," and knocked. My most endearing friend answered the door with her cute smile, and we embraced. I held on for a bit longer in hopes of giving her the chance saying she did not want to see me anymore. She didn't, was I glad for that, the first hurdle overcome. She noticed the plastic bag in my hand and questioned me about it. I told her it was a birthday gift for me and we could share it later. She acknowledged that and went back to the kitchen to finish up her kitchen duties. I knew what we were having for dinner and told her it smelled great. She replied, "It is all ready, come and get it." Who was I to not listen to her gentle request? As I entered the kitchen, I put the proposal on her chair in the living room. I entered the good smelling aroma of the apartment, pulled up a chair and stated the usual: "I'm hungry." We began the normal eating procedure, and I complimented her on the food. She talked about her day at work, and I imagined, this was going to be a forever thing, I couldn't wait, but I did. I finished up with my last bite as she was clearing the table. I don't eat as fast as the 'normal American'. I guess I'll live longer! We washed the dishes together, she in the water and me on the drying end. I put the towel away as she hung up the dishcloth and then came the moment of truth.

We walked into the living room. Of course she saw the plastic bag on her seat and asked, "What's this?" I paused for an instant and said, "It is my birthday present to you." She responded that it was my day and I was the one who got the gifts, not her. I replied that if she opened it and answered the question correctly, this will be <u>my</u> birthday present. With a puzzled look on her face, she opened my proposal poem. I watched her eyes, and as she read each line, she seemed to mist up a little, maybe that is what I wanted her to do. Then she finished the verse and read the first letter in each line, looked over the top of the frame and said, "Sure." She set the verse on the chair, came over the two steps it took to get to me, and we kissed the sweetest most passionate embrace I have ever tasted. Then we did it again, my forever kisses. What a pleasant thought to come home to every night, or her coming home to me.

Time To Buy The Rock

Now, came the time to purchase an engagement ring. I thought in my head that it might be best if we got it together. My dad has a friend, Fran, who has a shop right next door to his store, Loudy's Jewelry. They golfed every Wednesday, and they did the whole businessman thing. I had purchased several pieces of adornment there and he always gave us a fantastic price, much lower than other competitors in town. His jewelry was as good as or better than other stores. Over the years I have come to understand that life has many surprises within almost everything you do. I have prided myself in getting the most for my money.

We arrived at the parking lot behind Dad's store, got out and went to Loudy's through my dad's fabric business. As we greeted each of the clerks I grew up with, I told them of my intentions, and all shared in my happiness. I was only another man, ready to make a lifetime decision. We walked into his shop, paid our respects to the help, Mike and Lisa, greeted Fran and Mrs. Loudy. Fran walked back to his safe, got out a small black bag and brought it out to the main section of his shop. He loosened the top and emptied it.

As he proceeded to spill the glittering 'little rocks' onto his velvet pad, I swallowed; in fact, I gulped at the sight of these tiny, shining stars.

They ranged in size from .1 carat to as big as a marble. I wanted to buy the biggest one I could afford. We saw all of them under his magnifying lens. Mercy, they were gorgeous! No wonder the cost of these gems was so unimaginable I hadn't a clue as to their beauty. Mary Jo saw a diamond that she had all the intentions <u>my</u> purchasing. It was almost the size of a large marble. I then asked Fran the price.

He said it was $9500.00 I had to swallow a huge gulp of air and then said well if that's the one you want, it is okaywith me but we'll have to forget our first house and rent for the rest of our lives. No wonder wars and lives were won and lost over these rocks. But after all, they are only possessions in the whole scheme of things. But valuable, in the eyes of those who are into that type of need. We saw another beautiful stone that caught our attention. It was not very large, but it was exquisite in the way it looked, how it was cut—it was gorgeous from this humble man's point of view. I asked her if that was the one she desired and she nodded in excitement. Mary Jo looked up at me with her big brown eyes, misting a little at the corners, and said, "David, I love you!" I countered with I know, but, I love you more. We purchased the 'boulder' with a check, Fran told us when to pick it up, we asked if he might hurry, not that I was worried about the new situation but, I had to get her off the streets before she caught anyone else's attention. Like who would want me, except her? Maybe it was only my imagination, but I would have to think that way from now on. I am engaged. I had to think about this one for a while. A lifetime partner! Wow, I never thought anyone would even think of me as person to fall in love with and have a relationship to follow. After my accident, I thought

I probably would have to be a bachelor for my life here on planet earth: who needs the headache, heartache and puzzlement I would provide in their life. MARY JO DID! I fooled her, he he he!

Location, Location, Location

Where should we get married, New York or California? Mary Jo wanted to do the marriage thing in New York when the leaves started changing colors, the prettiest time of the year. I wanted to get married in California where all my kinfolk were. I guess I won because I was paying for the entire ceremony. I got what I wanted, the bride-to-be, she was the icing on my 'wedding cake'. We decided on California as the state where this blessed event would occur.

Now, came the wedding preparations. Good grief! All this hoopla for one day. We needed a church, food, music, and people to come to the occasion. I had plenty of people on my side, but most of her family and friends were to coming from back in New York and Hawaii and several of the states between.

We needed a church, our first obstacle. I thought of the church I went to in my younger days. I asked Mary Jo what she thought of this idea, a church, a non-denominational variety, where everyone would be satisfied. Actually the only ones we had to satisfy were each other and our Lord above, the Lord comes first.

We called and made an appointment to talk to the pastor and have Mary Jo look at the chapel from the inside. We arrived at the church on Dutton Avenue in San Leandro at 11:00 the morning of March 7, 1981. Pastor Hodges greeted us at the church door and invited us into God's house. He showed us around the entire chapel. I remembered most of it from my youth, the dark wood pews, the pulpit, the high arched ceiling and rafters, prettier than I once thought it to be. All I thought of was when was everything going to be over so I could go home and watch the ballgame on the television, so much for my old thoughts on religion. Mary Jo seemed to like the settings, the church scene and she agreed on the location. This was to be the place of the joining our lives. The pastor, during the two hours of discussion of our plans, told us he appreciated the fact that we had waited to wed longer than most couples. He also said he had a wonderful feeling that this union was going to last a long time. He stated that most of the younger couples he married didn't have as strong a determination of making it work as we did. I knew that has to be true, since we were both very near the thirty factor; she a little more and myself a bit less, but did it matter? Neither of us thought so, we only knew that it was right for both of us. If anyone disagreed it had to be their problem. Our love wasn't blind; it had its own boundaries.

Thank You For Sharing Your Day

We set the date for October 10, 1981. It was also my Granddad's 77th birthday. I thought he wouldn't mind sharing his day with us.

Now, we would need food to feed the masses. This was an important part of life, especially when you marry a young lady who, like me, loves to eat. We went to several caterers in the area where we tried out the cuisine of each one. We liked some but they were too expensive, others, the food was comparable to the hospital food I had 'enjoyed' in years past. Honestly, not the type of a meal I would want to serve my guests. It was a difficult part of the wedding process. I could hardly imagine what the next month could bring, who knows? We had a decent dinner delivered by Marie's catering in a nearby town, about three miles away for a fair price. We had them promise that they would supply the necessary food supplies to furnish our guests with a meal deserving their attention.

Mary Jo and her friend, Pat, did dried flowers and put them in old bottles as center pieces on each table, a touch different, but then look at the 'stars of the ceremony'. Pat also made the bride and groom characters out of bread dough. (We still have them and put them on our Christmas tree every year.) Not unlike the couple who were 'biting the dust' and were put on the top of the wedding cake. I could almost see them watching and laughing at all that was occurring at this blessed event.

I Just Love A Party Or Two Or Three...

Then it was party time! We had wedding showers, bridal showers and bachelor and bachelorette parties. All this hoopla happened over the next five months. Parties were thrown by my mother's friends, Nola and Leo Pickett, Mary Jo's sister, Barbara, who lived in Hayward. My newly added semi-brother, Aaron, from my stepfather's second wife's first marriage, threw a get-together for the occasion. What do you expect, we are from California! I realize that many divorces are unnecessary, but people are simply too caught up in the moment to understand what the 'D' word does to the child. That is why many people do get married so that they can reproduce and fulfill one of our Creator's wishes. Most children, even near-adult children, think it is their fault and they take the blame. I know I did many years ago.

I thought what Mary Jo and I did, by waiting a few years, sowing our wild oats, helped. I only had one or two, and they were 'oat flakes', but it all aided in strengthening the vows we would make to each other: it has worked so far! We decided, before we 'bit the dust', we were not going to have any children. In a way, I wanted a two or three but the medication, Dilantin, I was on to control my seizures made me think twice about what could happen to the unborn child my wife would have carried. That is all we need, to bring another disabled child into the world. His or her disabled father would be more than enough of a burden in this sometimes cruel, ugly world. So, it took a great deal of explanation when we informed the grandparents that there were not going to be any great grandkids by way of David and Mary Jo. They told us how selfish we were to deprive them the joy of not having any great grandkids to spoil. We asked them if they wanted great-grandchildren, would they like to purchase our first home for us in this wonderful world in which we reside? After all, financially we could not afford the cost of both. Then, we simply hushed up, took their mean-spirited way of trying to spoil my beautiful new addition to our family, my wife-to-be, Mary Jo. So much for choices in this big world around us, after all, it was our decision and ours alone. We are going to be the ones to have to answer to our Creator, no one else.

Then, there was Barbara, my sister-in-law-to-be's, kitchen creations time. Over a dozen female neighbors from around her block came. They brought gifts concerning one of my favorite rooms, the kitchen. Mary Jo received towels, dishcloths, recipe books, kitchen tools, pots and pans. Everything she got was appreciated. The reason for the kitchen shower was we already had everything we needed. We had accumulated almost all that gear prior to our engagement, because we merged two separate households. I loved duplicate kisses and hugs are never too much. I guess I am only a simple man with simple thoughts about life and what is necessary to have a full and meaningful way of living. But that is only David, a unique type of person who requires very little, except being wanted and needed. The best thing about that evening, I was the only man in the group. I was nearly a king for the evening, what a wonderful short-lived memory. I am not a male chauvinist pig, but I am not a weakling either. I have my own point of view ...... don't I dear? And I am not even married yet, can you imagine what it will be like if...... I don't even want to think about it.

Gussying Up

Then we had to get our wedding clothes. Mary Jo needed a dress, not a gown, and I would wear a rented fancy suit. Not a tuxedo, that was much too ritzy for our humble affair.

Mary Jo, her sister Barbara, and my mom, Doris, went to Gunny Sac; a fine ladies clothiers in San Francisco. They shopped to pick out a dress for this once-in-a-lifetime occasion. She tried on three dresses, then thought she would find a better deal at another store. She liked the first dress she tried on, but she had to get the best deal for her money; I think it must be a woman's way of thinking . . . oink! oink! oink! She was frugal and that was one of her finest selling points. She went to two other shops in search of the best deal, and she ended up going back to Gunny Sac and purchased the first dress she saw and liked. So much for better deals, go with the heart, not the pocketbook. Her dress cost a grand total of...$75.00. Did she get a deal or what? Much to my mom and Barbara's dismay, this shopping trip was short lived.

She would not let me see her choice of dresses before the wedding even though I knew the tale about seeing the outfit before the day was supposed to be bad luck. I also knew that she had 'pretty' good taste in most everything, so I did not worry about her taste in clothes. I did have some concern in her taste in men. Not really, in my eyes, I was the one for her and she was the one for me. Ain't love grand! Or blind? But, it was going to work, I planned that I was only going to do this once, and once is all you need if it is done right. Of course there will be problems everyone faces, but it is how you handle these difficulties that will determine your fate. If you let your mate take a controlling position instead of working out the problems that you face together, you more than likely will not be as happy or content with the results; 'united we stand'. I don't like to preach, but if I am asked about a situation, I will offer my opinion no questions asked, you may not like what I have to say, but you asked.

Now it was my turn to get all fixed up. I needed to ask Mary Jo at least the color of her dress, white, beige, black; after all it was my funeral. She replied that it was an off-white/beige lace with an empire waistline. I had to get a compatible matching outfit, only not in white. My semi-newly acquired brother, Aaron, was to be my best man. He and I went to BIG AND TALL CLOTHIERS in San Leandro at Bay Fair shopping center. We walked in and talked to the clerk and said we needed to rent four fancy tan/brownish almost-tuxedos for the upcoming event on October 10. The reason we needed four suits was because Mary Jo's oldest brother and her dad, from New York, were also in the wedding party. He told us that there would be no problem. I felt like I was a little kid in a clothing factory as I looked at all fancy 'duds' they had to offer. Aaron was almost as bad as me, but he wasn't the one who was walking down the plank . . . glub glub. Thank goodness I had taken some of the swimming lessons we need to survive in this game of life. I am so appreciative of my folks and my upbringing, they did a pretty good job, considering.

We picked out a light brown suit with a vest and dark shoes and tried them on. I looked pretty good for a brain-traumatized young man and so did Aaron, for a younger-than-me kid brother. I never had a brother who I could confide in and tell him my fantasies as well as the truths about what I was actually feeling. It felt very comfortable talking to him. It was almost as though we really were brothers. He is more mature than most, losing his dad at a very young age helped in his psychological development. Then we got the receipt for the suits rental and the promise that they would have the clothes ready and promptly when we picked them up on October 8, two days before the wedding.

We left the store confident and feeling great about the upcoming event. Though I was a touch nervous, I suppose most everyone feels the same way; this too shall pass, and it did. I knew I shouldn't be afraid of my new venture, heck, I thought everybody did it and it always turned out good. Then I remembered, oops! Look at my parents and their parents, what occurred to make them split? Was it the lack of faith, the need to stray, money, the change of life? Whatever it was, it would never happen to ours. This was probably a desire of all of the un-marrieds, worldwide.

Indecisions... Not Me

We headed home and talked about the upcoming event. Aaron questioned me about my decision. Was I sure? Will it last? And why? were some of his inquiries. I told him it was going to be great, everyone has difficulties, but when you talk with our GOD above, he will guide and direct you. He understood what I was telling him. He was a good kid and I loved him, even though he was just a nineteen-year-old youth, he was still my BEST man. No one could ever replace him. Dad made a good choice in picking another wife and also Aaron's mother Patty was lovely. She is more than another woman in my dad's life, she brought out some qualities I never thought he had in him, and she is special!

He dropped me off at my apartment, shook hands, hugged and he said, "Sweet dreams." He knew I would have a few problems getting to sleep that night and every night until my 'execution day', the day I would lose my bachelor status and join the ranks of the married but not buried in this new life l was about to enter. We knew everything was going to turn out as perfect as was to be expected.

Practice Makes Perfect

Next was the rehearsal for the upcoming event. The church where we were to get married hadn't changed in umpteen years. Mary Jo's family arrived in bits and pieces, coming from all over the country; including Hawaii, San Diego, and her home state of New York where the majority of her people lived. Her out-of-state brothers and sisters stayed with family and most of mine were already here or close enough to go home right after our blessed event.

The big day was closely approaching and it just so happened I was getting a touch nervous. Do I truly want to go through with this? I guess I am committed (or maybe should be. NAH!) I made a promise to myself, that once you give your word, you hold to it, after all a promise is a promise. I learned that in kindergarten. Besides, there is a thing called love, an extremely strong emotion that makes many men do the darndest things. Marriage is included in that list, as I look back, it is probably on the top. I am extremely happy that I didn't do anything crazy, like take a vacation to Tahiti!

The wedding party met at the chapel, with the people involved, and were in great spirits for the upcoming event except the stars of the show. They were as nervous as two lambs going to slaughter. Well, maybe I am exaggerating a touch, but we had never done anything like this before. All of this was new and uncharted territory for us to enter into, but like Columbus, we took the chance. I knew I was going to win, at least I was sure. I had already won her heart over, now was the time to make everything upright and legal. Pastor Hodges brought the people together and started giving directions about the upcoming event and what was going to occur.

First of all, he took us to the church's front door where the people would enter and sign the guest book. The ushers, Joe and Mike, my brother-in-laws-to-be, would escort all the ladies, young and old, into the church, asking them bride or groom's side. Her brother Michael was needed as an extra usher. He did not have a rented suit like her brother Joe. So much for the perfect wedding details!

The majority of the people were my family and friends. I would have three-fourths of the guests sitting on my side of the chapel, and Mary Jo had the rest, about thirty. It wasn't like I had more friends; they just lived closer to the church. Even though the day was supposed to be the bride's big day, in all actuality, it was mainly <u>my</u> day. I felt that I wanted to show off the greatest accomplishment I had done by finding a woman who loved and cared enough for me. We made one of the first compromises with many more to come in this fine institution called marriage. Mary Jo never wanted a big a splashy gathering. She told me she would be happy going to Reno and getting hitched. No one ever thought that David Seymon would even get married. Who would want that poor, sorry disabled person? It so happened that this one unassuming young lady with a kind and loving heart, did not pity anything except homeless cats and other wild creatures. She truly did care enough, and I guess I am a bit of a wild thing, at least to her and she is the only thing that matters to me.

Then Pastor Hodges brought us into the main church where the blessed event was to occur. It brought back memories of my baptism and quietly laughing or giggling at what was going on at peoples' weddings, church services and other Sunday occasions. I envisioned the walk up the carpeted aisle like a stroll down the yellow brick road hoping to see the great and almighty wizard asking him to marry this humble couple. Then reality set in as I looked at my lovely wife-to-be. She was smiling and looking my way; I thought she was checking out the church and maybe even saying to herself, is this the right thing to do? She blinked, smiled to herself, then seemed to nod it was okay. This, in my eyes, meant she was at peace with the whole marriage idea. I knew I was. I never had any doubts about this whole thing, I was pleased and confident that Mary Jo accepted me for who I was, what I might be like over the next decade or two.

The pastor had us get into the correct positions for our practice betrothal. Mary Jo was behind door number one and I was positioned with my best man, Aaron, in front of the altar. The organist started the ceremony going with a pre-wedding song, "We've Only Just Begun," and things started to proceed as intended. I was standing, waiting for my bride-to-be to stroll out of door number one and begin her walk up the aisle. I have come to realize that New Yorkers do not stroll, they walk everywhere at warp speed (unlike we Californians, who do not do anything fast unless it endangers our lives or it is time to eat or fall in love). Then again, I am the exception to all those rules. I enjoy being unique and so does Mary Jo.

She was extremely attractive in her blue jeans and cotton top, but I was not that much better in my faded baby blues and white cotton dress shirt. I was nothing to brag about either, did we care? I don't think so. We just wanted to get this whole thing over and done so we could get on with our new life of living together. Her dad was at her side, being as proud as a father could be. Mary Jo and Papa Joe had a special relationship. I almost sensed this closeness that only certain family members contain. I know there was no such similar bonding in my family as in theirs. I was little bit envious of the fact, but such is life. As she paraded down the aisle towards me, I became a bit nervous to the fact that my bachelor days were nearing their end. I was anxious and a little mixed up (my semi-normal state). I was so pleased that I had found the right woman who would take me as I was and turn me into the man I was meant to be. I always considered myself a whole person until the time of my accident. That mishap changed my whole perspective on the life I led in my disabled body, so much for outward appearances. My thought is: to be happy on the outside, one must be content with themselves on the inside, playground psychology. People are too concerned with how good looking your date is, rather than what is going on inside their heart. I lost my heart the first time I spoke with my "date." She was well-spoken, kind and just plain fun to be around. I snatched her right out from under the noses of those other possible guys who might have had other 'thoughts' concerning their needs. I needed her more than any of them and I won the prize.

Mary Jo arrived near my side with a little twinkle in her eye. After she and her father embraced, they turned towards me and he put her hand into mine. I took it as gently as I could and gave it a tiny squeeze. We looked into each other's eyes, I winked and asked her, in my way of doing things, if she was okay with everything, and she winked back. I love it when girls wink at you. It doesn't usually happen to me but when she winked back it seemed to make my whole life's dream finally come true. The pastor started his marital presentation to a small group of persons who wanted to see this loving couple join the ranks of the married.

Pastor Hodges started the wedding routine with his introduction of what he was going to say, how we were to react to each question he would venture our way, and the best part of the evening, our 'forever kiss'. I tried to make mental notes of what was to take place. It was a little difficult at first to grasp everything all at once, but I treated it like I do a poem. I got an idea, thinking where I wanted to go with this thought, then, putting it down on paper. My mind was the pad, so that everyone will enjoy the punch line, our saying, "I DO." The pastor had Mary Jo go to the back of the chapel where she was to enter the doors when the music started. My best man, Aaron and I, waited at the altar. She started up the aisle in her New York fashion, walking up the carpet like she had no sense of rhythm, a faster type beat than all the rest of participants were listening to. She made it to the preacher in record time, leaving the rest of the wedding party in the dust. The preacher tried to tell Mary Jo that the race to the altar would be won when the two of us said the two best-known words in the English language. She agreed and told him she was only a bit nervous and would try to slow the whole process down to a minor roar. As I stood there smiling at the entire scene, I had found prior to this event, say in the first few minutes of our relationship, that Mary Jo is an AA-type personality. That means that she does all her life's motions at warp speed times two. She listened to him with her reluctant New York ears and slowed way down, for the moment. She did not try it again; the pastor thought it would work out. The wedding party stood at the altar facing the pastor and waiting for his gentle words. He did a short mock service in which we read our own self-written vows. It made me think, do I really want to go through with this? You bet I do, and I can hardly wait, but all good things happen to those who do wait. I heard him and did everything he told us to do, but I was so impatient all I wanted to do was grab Mary Jo and take her to the nearest judge, have him pronounce us man and wife, and get this whole thing over with. What a selfish idea! There is a young person, still inside of me, trying to take over my 'nearly normal' 29-year-old exterior and do a ridiculous notion like that. We continued the 'practice wedding', promising this and promising that. I knew in my heart what was correct in all I wanted to do, have, and need. I thought the whole thing would be easier than it was. I have come to the conclusion that everything in life worth waiting for. It takes as much time as it needs to come to fruition. So it was time to hold my horses, count to ten and ponder until it was my turn to say those words I had practiced in front of my mirror at my apartment in San Leandro for months on end, 'I dill', 'I woo', 'let me talk it over with my broker'. Amen.

Mary Jo and I joined hands as we listened to Pastor Hodges talk to us, this couple who were about to make a lifetime commitment. Forever seemed like such a long time. Marriage is a large part of this thing we know as life. It is only as good as the parties involved and how they handle each situation placed in front of them. If they have trouble finding the right decision, they must go for help, whether it be earthly aid or heavenly help.

Pastor Hodges started the 'pre-marriage vows', the words we would have to think about for the next two days. Prior to the rehearsal, we wrote our own vows and had them ready to recite as soon as the pastor gave us the cue. We then said our 'practice vows'. It was a little funny to make all these statements of our love. I knew in my heart that this marriage was not only for thrill of it for the time at hand, it was going to be for the rest of my life. I made the correct choice in finding a mate who I could trust for the rest of my days and I am sure she felt the same about me. This brain-traumatized man was totally convinced of his love and affection for this little woman as she approached this altar, in front of Our Lord to make a pledge of eternal commitment.

Rehearsal Dinner

On October 8, again, Barbara fed the whole lot of us, she must be a saint. We ate, talked, and carried on for half the night. There were only two who sat in nervous anticipation of the upcoming event, the 'semi-stars' of the show. We picked at our food. The turkey and ham did not go to waste, though, only most of the people who were there watched it go to their waists, while over indulging in Barbara's wonderful cuisine.

It was a stroke of luck my becoming the newest member of the Schmieg family. The amazing part to me, even being the new addition, was the fact that they did not belittle me or make fun of me or even make me the heel of their jokes. They accepted me as I was, David, the human being. I was considered just like all the rest of the 'tribe', only a bit limited in some of the things I was able to accomplish.

They knew that when I was introduced, we were together. The whole family regarded me as one of them, no questions asked. I actually felt that I was somebody who was a whole somebody. Love is good, even if it comes to you in a way other than the "normal expected way." Some members of my kinfolk were not as accepting as my family-to-be. I have trouble understanding their thinking. I knew I was 'half adopted', but, I was so young when I was adopted. I was the oldest of three children, and I did not even consider that they would make me the laughingstock of many of their jokes. I have come to understand that my love and respect for them, appeared to me, to mean nothing, so why did I even try to gain theirs? *Love should not be earned. If merited, it should be given with a warm, accepting and open heart.* I was never good at earning merit badges.

Being with the Schmiegs is good, like the love I gave to them in return. I have come to realize that marrying a young lady from New York of German/Italian descent was the best thing I could have ever wanted to accomplish in my life. I welcomed her with wide-open arms. Her kindness attracted me, her acceptance overwhelmed me and her love secured our relationship.

Now began the final preparation for the BIGGEST event in my life, ever! I was a bit nervous about the whole thing, actually I was nearly petrified. When this brain trauma victim goes into a situation where I am a complete beginner, my thought process gets scattered, and in my case, I get confused. Confusion is one of my favorite states to visit, though I would <u>not</u> want to live there.

Two More Days

I came back to my secure apartment, a place I had called home for almost six years, opened the door and started talking to the walls. I have never talked to these walls or any other part of the building ever! This was odd, could this be a part of marriage I had never heard about or was it only another part of the brain damage game I had been playing for the past eleven years? I have come to realize that it was plain, old nerves. What, me nervous, no way!

I called my mom as she asked (the over protective mother thing!) don't cha just love it…. she told me that there was a little pre-wedding thing going on at her place and of course I was invited. I guess I am a bit of a ham when the limelight is shining in my direction. I went to her place and had what appeared to be "the final single meal ala my mom." Of course it was delicious and her dessert was stupendous. Dessert is the favorite part of any meal as far as I am concerned. I thanked her for her preparation of my final meal as a single young man.

Back to my apartment, a most secure place to be in this life-changing time. I undressed, hopped into a wonderfully warm shower and started scrubbing away. I brushed my teeth, applied my night creams, took my daily dose of those dreaded, dulling, but most-needed seizure medications. Next, I put on my pajamas, stuck my body in between my sheets and blankets, and spoke with our Father above. I asked him to make sure that the day after tomorrow would be the finest day of my life. Then, I closed my eyes, thinking, *what a wonderful life I am going to lead.* I drifted off into Never-Never Land. I was ready for my new set of struggles and adventures; this B.T. individual was soon to become the United States' newest married man.

I slept most of the night but woke up on occasion in deep thought about this new life I was about to enter. Everything was going to change from the 'me version' to the becoming 'us style of living'. What a night! I woke up early, called Aaron, my brother and best man and told him how great I felt about this marriage idea. He brought over our rented suits, and we dressed in our fancy attire. It is always slow for me. Aaron saw what Mary Jo was getting into. He knew about my 'non-speed' way of doing things, since he had been my brother for several years. We had known each other long before this marriage thing came into being. We talked; he asked me questions about the changes I would go through. All this planning we had done for the past several months would only be pleasant memory. I told him to watch us and how, with our Lord's help, it all works out the best for everyone involved. We finished putting on our fancy 'duds' then I looked in the mirror and said, "Is this for real?" Do I know what I am doing? I guess it was just the premarital jitters as many of my friends told me what to expect. The only thing is, they were not in my shoes and most of them had done it at least twice. In my heart, I knew my marriage would last forever, with the help of our dear friend above. The two of us knew the truth about how to live, the way our Lord taught us. We looked at each other and checked things out. He noticed that my tie was crooked and I saw one of his sleeves was shorter than the other. I compared this to two monkeys picking bugs off each other's hides. Then, all of a sudden out of the blue, Aaron put on an ugly face, started grunting and throwing one of his hands under his armpit and started scratching. I cracked up and said, "Oh my goodness we are on the same on the same wavelength. I was comparing us to chimpanzees also then you did that, what a shock!" I asked, "Aaron, how long have we known each other?"Aaron retorted, "Too long". I replied, "Brother, not long enough." We hugged, then started to get ready to go to the church. We hopped into his Mustang, and en-route we talked and talked, a nervous gabbing of one who is on the way to a new beginning. Aaron was a young pup who was not aware of the finality of this big step that his older brother was about to do. From 163rd we went right down East 14th Street all the way to Dutton Avenue. We turned right again then up six blocks to Dowling Boulevard, where the Congregational Church building was located. We were a little bit early, that is something for me. After my accident, my dad always told me I would be late for my own funeral, and I almost proved him wrong once and I was not going to finally make him right. The church looked ominous, since it was an old structure of plaster and wood all done in a Victorian style. It waited to consume its next victims of love, who needed to tie the eternal 'not' (knot).

We exited the Mustang, me a lot slower than my brother, again, the normal thing, and went in the front door of the church. I was approaching the 'excited stage' of this event. We gazed at the inside of this antiquated edifice, admiring the ornate design of every pillar holding up the roof and sides. All I knew was that I would have to be Mary Jo's pillar for the rest of our natural days. If I was any kind of husband, I would do so to the best of my abilities. We saw Pastor Hodges in the front of the chapel doing his 'getting ready for the marriage thing'. He was straightening up his collar and putting the final touches on the altar. This is where we were to say the marriage vows we wrote and practiced over and over. Approaching him, we greeted him and I told him, "I am the male half of the couple you are going to marry today." He smiled and said, "You appear to be the naturally more nervous one of the two, so of course you are." He then took us to the husband-to-be's 'chamber room' where all good pre-husbands wait for their time to arrive. We went into the tiny room where there was a mirror, sink, and bathroom fixture.

We cautiously opened the door a crack to see if anyone was entering the chapel. Ms. Mick from Fairmont Hospital was one of the first to arrive. Slowly others entered the place where I was going to make my final stand as a single male. I readied myself for the marital oath I was about to make in front of my wife-to-be, friends, family and our Lord above. Again, I was bitten by that bug of nerves. I should have been cool, calm, and collected, like all semi-young men who are about to give up their last breath of single freedom. I had fallen prey to a New York young lady who ended up stealing my heart and all of the love that it contained—a wise choice on my part.

I had love to share. The thing I found most unique was that the church was almost overflowing on my pew side and Mary Jo had about thirty people from what seemed like everywhere across the map.

I spoke to Aaron in a nervous tone of voice saying am I truly biting the dust or is this only a façade. As the people entered the chapel, the part of me that wanted to get this whole thing over and done with was growing and another part of me wanted it to last forever. For now, I will stick to the forever part, I love parties. The wedding setting was almost ready to be put in place. Aaron and I came out of the room nearest the altar and stood awaiting my bride to come out of the doorway in the rear of the church. Rev. Hodges signaled the organist to begin the famous tune, which draws the bride to the groom's side. The doors opened slowly, out came Barbara in her off-white, floor length bridesmaid's dress. Her lovely sister Ann followed, all in perfect time with the music. Then came the star attraction, the one I fell madly in love with, my lifetime-partner-to-be, Mary Jo. She made her way into the limelight. She was hanging onto her father's arm, like a puppy being given away to a new owner; she did not seem to want to leave. As she approached me, I could see that ol' mist in her eyes and it was trickling down her cheeks. She was almost at my side when she and her 'misty-faced' dad faced each other and kissed a soft, sweet, endearing, and what appeared to be farewell kiss. I thought to myself, you are not losing a daughter; you are gaining another son-in-law, how lucky can you get? He gently placed her hand in mine and gave me another "boy, how lucky can you get, taking one of my favorite daughters, you better be good to her" look. My smile thanked him for the opportunity of joining him while entering their family.

We turned and faced the pastor. I was grinning the entire time during my wait for the pastor to begin the final chapter of my bachelor days. I was waiting for the words, "Dearly beloved we are gathered here today," but I did not hear them. He started with, "We are here to join in matrimony this fine couple, who came to realize that their love must be knotted together in this joint venture called marriage. This is a perfect solution for children of our Lord with intentions of making a new and better life. Both of them now become one in His eyes."

He then let us recite our vows we wrote for this marriage thing.

I started with:

> Mary Jo, I pledge my life to you,
> to love and support in all you do.
> I will be with you all of my life,
> together we stand in good times and strife.
> I promise to listen, I promise to care,
> and with GOD'S help, I will always be there.

Then Mary Jo sheepishly smiled at me and I grinned back, all in anticipation of stating her vows to me, she sweetly said:

David, I pledge my life to you,
to love and support in all you do.
I will be with you all of my life,
together, we stand in good times and strife.
I promise to listen, I promise to care,
and with GOD'S help, I will always be there.

Pastor Hodges asked if anyone had any objections to this marriage. No one said a word. He stated that since there were none, he now pronounced us husband and wife. A hundred thoughts raced through my mind, why didn't anyone object? What do I do now? What have I gotten myself into? Where is the back door? Then reality set in, guess what David, you are married!

The fine pastor then said five of my most favorite words in the entire English language, "YOU MAY KISS THE BRIDE"!

I said to myself, "I don't want to make a spectacle of the situation placed before us," so I looked at her, saw her quiver a little, put my arms out and softly around her. Our eyes met, then, closed, our lips slowly approached and met. This must be the first forever kiss of the marriage, and I want more of these. I remembered what the Good Book says, "All good comes to those who wait." So it was a gentle, soft kiss. More views of what lay ahead again sped within my head. *I love this woman more than life itself and now we are finally a pair.* We turned toward the congregation and Pastor Hodges proudly announced and introduced the newest married couple in all of California, David and Mary Jo. We slowly walked down the aisle, and the wedding watchers clapped in approval of this new union of body and soul. I was so proud of my wife I could hardly control myself, but I did.

Reception Time

Then came the pictures and the pictures and more pictures, I felt as if I was a movie star...t. The only thing I wasn't asked for was my autograph. We moved on to the reception where everyone was waiting for the newly hitched pair to come enjoy the food, music and festivities. After thanking everyone who came, we sat down at the head table and waited for our food. As we were served first, everyone seemed to be at peace with each other, shaking hands, hugging and enjoying the entire occasion, but not as much as me. Aaron, my brother, gave the toast for this happening, blessing our union and wishing us many years of 'honeymoonal' bliss. In my mind, I knew it would last a long, long time. Love is good just like the people involved.

We finished our wedding supper and then the music started. We had a song that we enjoyed both the sound and the meaning of the words. It was "I Made It Through The Rain." After the solo dance where the 'dynamic duo' do their thing in front of the whole wedding party, the parents barged in so they could get in the pictures. Then came the money dance. Mary Jo cleaned up making about $375.00. My mother's date, Ed, pinned two $100.00 bills on my new wife's bosom. She was as shocked as was I when I saw them but it was a very, 'very rich sight to behold'. Boy was she lucky! I was not that fortunate, I only got a $20.00 stuck in my belt. I ended up with $150.00. I have always told her that she was prettier than me and this was the proof.

We danced and carried on for about half an hour, then it was the garter belt-bouquet toss time. Mary Jo came over to a chair, sat her cute little torso down, crossed her legs, and pulled up her gown, but not too high. Being the bashful one that I am, I did not want to have my new wife expose too much of her newly-claimed private property. Was I a prude or what? I took my own sweet time removing her garter belt, and the band played on. I got the 'nasty' piece of lingerie off her lovely leg, stood up, looked around the room for my brother in hopes of his catching it. I turned my back to the unmarried men in the group, stretched the rubbery piece of undergarment, pulling it back as far as I could. Just as I was going to let it fly, I gripped the end of it and faked some of them out, not all, but enough to get a moan out of the crowd. I then turned my back again and let it fly. It streaked through the air and it was the perfect garter toss, right into Aaron's hand. Were we good or what?

Then Mary Jo took her bouquet and turned around, 1 – 2 – 3, reared back and sent it flying. The young ladies, who, at this time, did not appear that ladylike, scrambled for the bridal bouquet. Out of nowhere came the hands of Colleen, a friend of hers from work, who had 'immigrated' from back east. She snatched the flowers in mid-air like a wide receiver grabbing the football for a winning touchdown; sign that girl up.

The photographer got pictures of everything, from the tosses to the grabs of the prized possessions. I got my prized possession when I found, captured, and married my little New York young lady friend.

Things started to slow down a bit and we got ready to leave the church, off to that thing called the honeymoon. We headed toward the church's front door, slowly making our way through all of the well-wishers, applauders and parents. We opened the front door of the church, went outside and through all of the rice being thrown, there was my new wife's 1966 Pontiac Catalina waiting to carry us back to Mary Jo's apartment house. We had the usual tin cans tied onto the bumper, a few honking horns, and several friends in their cars. Again I must say, isn't love grand? We went down East14th Street past the stores and people I had met and known over the many years I lived in my fair city. I was so pleased and proud that had I found the love of my life, caught, and finally married her. And there I sat with a smile hanging from my ears with my arm surrounding my new bride, knowing this was the happiest day of my life.

After The Bash

We arrived at her apartment, got out and progressed to her front door. I picked her up and carried her across the threshold into her apartment. This would be our life's new home in about five days, after the honeymoon. We got out of the wedding apparel and into something much more comfortable, blue jeans and casual tops. Mom and Ed came and picked us up and took us to San Francisco. We ate dinner at the Tonga Room in the Fairmont Hotel. What great food and service we received. What a wonderful beginning for newlyweds and their life's journey. After dinner, we went to the 'honeymoon hotel', the Sheraton, near the San Francisco airport.

We entered the lobby and went straight to the front desk. We told them our names, her new one and mine. The bell person quickly rushed to our side pushing his luggage cart. I thought to myself, do we appear to be rookies of this new lifestyle?

Probably so, I could never fake anything; especially the love I have for my new wife, did I say wife? It was starting to hit me. I had joined the group of 'married but not buried', duos who go through life, 'attached at the hip', so to speak.

He brought our luggage up to our honeymoon room. We entered the room, looked at all the fancy amenities. I had never stayed in such a plush hotel in my entire life. I am a 'Motel 6' kind of guy. So call me cheap; I consider myself thrifty. I looked at everything in the room, but I took a good look at the object of my dreams since the day that I met her in our poetry class almost two years ago. I guess it is true, some things do improve with age, and she was one of them. I approached her, took her hand, brought it to my shoulder, leaned down and gently kissed her on her cheek. I told her how much she meant to me and that I loved every inch of her body. She whispered, show me. I sped, that's a joke, over to the hotel door, removed the do not disturb sign hanging from the inside and placed it on the outside handle …….. and closed the door.

Sealed With A Kiss

My friendship turned to love in a matter of a few days.
Being around her brought sunshine with warming rays.
This growing emotion had no bounds,
I gave her the heart that my loves surrounds.

The days flew past as this story is told,
I worked up the courage and then I got cold.
Giving her a proposal in a special poem form,
I waited nervously, as my emotions did swarm.

She gave me the nod, my ideas ran wild,
How could she handle, this man who's a child.
I grew up quick, as fast as I could,
With their support, everyone knew I would.

So, betrothal plans were made by this fine pair,
Many had doubts, but in my mind, they were rare.
Get-togethers and parties, which seemed not to end,
My strong love for her, she could always depend.

With the wedding date approaching, everything was set,
I was so proud about the day that we had met,
The time was upon us, it had come quite fast,
For a lifetime commitment that forever will last.